THE
POWER
OF
SERVING
OTHERS

YOU CAN START
WHERE YOU ARE

GARY MORSCH and
DEAN NELSON

dustjacket

The Power of Serving Others
Second Edition/Paperback

Dust Jacket Press
P.O. Box 721243
Oklahoma City, OK 73172
www.dustjacket.com

Ordering information for print editions:
Quantity sales. Special discounts are available on quantity purchases by corporations, associations, and others. For details, contact the Dust Jacket Press address above.

Individual sales. Dust Jacket Press publications are available through most bookstores. They can also be ordered directly from Dust Jacket: Tel: (800) 495-0192; Email: info@ dustjacket.com; www.dustjacket.com

Dust Jacket logos are registered trademarks of Dust Jacket Press, Inc.

Design and production: Doug West; Dust Jacket Creative Services
Cover design: Richard Adelson

Printed in United States of America

www.dustjacket.com

To our wives, Vickie and Marcia, who, when we think of you,
make us want to paraphrase Louis Armstrong and sing,

"And we think to ourselves, what a wonderful world!"

CONTENTS

PREFACE

Look again at the book's cover. The hand is holding something that is going to grow. Even though it is small right now, its roots will go deep and its branches will spread. It will provide strength or shade or beauty to its surroundings. It could grow in a yard or a forest, but it will grow because that is what it is meant to do. And, as it grows, it will change the world around it.

This book is about changing our world. It's not about a revolution, but it *is* revolutionary.

It's about serving others—looking at others as people who could use a hand. It's about looking at our hands and realizing that they already contain what others need.

This book starts with some assumptions—mainly that people really do want to help one another and make the world better, but they often don't know how to do it. It also assumes that people are looking for meaning and significance in their lives, but they don't know how to find them. They've tried accumulating wealth, tried increasing excitement, tried exercising authority, but those attempts left them empty. The book assumes that people are asking, What am I here for? It assumes we're searching for something and don't know where to look.

This book shows that the answers to life's important questions are simple, but not easy.

This is a book that claims something extraordinary: That the true source of power in our lives, the power to change the world, is available when we serve others. I have seen this firsthand through the impact of Gary Morsch's life and Heart to Heart International, the humanitarian relief agency he started.

Our paths crossed a few times in the 1970s and 1980s, but it was not until 1991 that Gary and I had our first deep conver- sation. He was in New York for a board meeting for the Lamb's Club, an arts, community service, and ministry center just off Times Square. I was in New York, working on a project with *The New York Times*. I had rented an apartment at the Lamb's Club, just a block or two from the Times building.

One night some of the Lamb's board members were going to see *The Grapes of Wrath* at a Broadway theater and they invited me to join them. I had always been moved by the story of the Joads, leaving one desperate situation after another as they moved from Oklahoma to California during the Dust Bowl. I was particularly struck by the ending where, just as it looked as if no one had anything left, they found a way to help someone even more desperate than themselves.

When the show was over, most of our group headed for the subway, but Gary and I walked back to the Lamb's together. We got to talking about what we wanted to do with our lives. I told Gary I wanted to write about things that mattered. He told me he wanted to figure out a way to help suffering people. He thought there must be a way to take excess resources and match them with people who need them. We ended up walking through late-night New York for hours.

"I think that, deep down inside, people truly want to help others," he said. "They just don't know how. Wouldn't it be something to match the desires of those people with the needs of the world?"

It was too big a concept for me to get my brain around, but I remember thinking "If you could figure that out, I'd love to write about it."

Since then, Gary started Heart To Heart International, a humanitarian relief organization, and linked thousands of vol- unteers who have the desire to serve others with people who desperately need assistance. Annually, Heart to Heart International assists 250 organizations with over $100 million in humanitarian aid and supplies. This level of assistance has created strong partnerships with major Fortune 500 companies and the largest pharmaceutical companies in the world. Named to Forbes magazine's prestigious list of "America's 200 Largest Charities", HHI is also recognized as one of the leaders in donor efficiency and charitable commitment. HHI has intentionally maintained a lean and highly efficient organization with 98% of all contributions going directly to relief and development programs – all administrative and fundraising activities are supported by less than 2% of total contributions.

Volunteers are the key—people wanting to help others. What I have observed about the people who volunteer is that their eyes open to the needs in their own neighborhoods and communities, even in their own homes, and serving others becomes part of their lifestyle. They see the power available to change the way they view the world, others, and themselves.

One of the biggest transformations I observed was that, when people began to serve others, they saw how easy it was to start wherever they were, regardless of their circumstances and resources.

We don't have to go to different parts of the world to serve. We can serve the person we encounter next.

That's the conclusion I hope you reach when you read this book.

This is the second book Gary Morsch and I have written together. The first, Heart and Soul: Awakening Your Passion to Serve (Beacon Hill Press of Kansas City, 1997), told of the early years of Heart to Heart and some of the miraculous events that allowed the organization to become so life-changing for so many people. I recommend it, because it will astound, encourage and inspire you.

As we were finishing this book, Hurricane Katrina struck New Orleans and the surrounding area. We got into New Orleans before many of the relief workers, and saw first-hand how badly we need each other, and how willing others are to help. Gary and I saw the lessons of this book come alive one more time in that storm.

The Power of Serving Others articulates the personal philosophies of both Gary and me. Most experiences narrated being specifically Gary's, we made the decision to write the book entirely in his voice. There are two authors, but one editorial voice. It's like two musicians, singing in unison.

Look at the book's cover again. As you read this book you'll see how that plant can grow and sense your own purpose grow- ing right along with it.

Dean Nelson
San Diego, California

ACKNOWLEDGMENTS

This book is the embodiment of the message within it—that serving others begins where we are. Mindi McKenna of Kansas City heard us talk about serving others, and she served us by offering to open a door to Ken Blanchard. Ken then introduced us to Martha Lawrence, a superb editor, who encouraged us and told us we had a message that needed to be heard. Martha introduced us to Steve Piersanti of Berrett-Koehler Publishing Co. Steve pushed and prodded and challenged us to make the message better, and Berrett-Koehler published the first edition of this book. This is the second edition. Thank you Mindi, Ken, Martha, and Steve.

Both of us have spouses who understand the meaning of serving others. In many respects, they taught us how to serve. Books like this take a long time to gather information and to write. That often comes at the great personal expense of time together. So, Vickie and Marcia, thank you for seeing the value in this project, and thank you for understanding the time it took to produce.

Gary Morsch and
Dean Nelson

INTRODUCTION

ASK THE QUESTION

The ultimate aim of the quest must be neither release nor ecstasy for oneself, but the wisdom and the power to serve others.

Joseph Campbell[1]

In Leo Tolstoy's short story "What Men Live By," an impoverished shoemaker encounters a naked man freezing to death on a Russian winter night. It turns out that the naked man is an angel who disobeyed God. He had been ordered by God to take the soul of a dying woman, but his action would have left two orphaned children; the angel did not want to carry out his instruction. The woman died anyway, and the angel was banished from heaven until he could find answers to three questions on earth: What is given to men? What is not given to men? What do men live by?

Through the compassion of the shoemaker and his wife, the angel learned the answer to the first question: What is given to men? *Love is given to all people, and dwells in their hearts.*

Through a boastful and demanding rich man, the angel learned the answer to the second question: What is not given to men? The man had ordered fancy boots, but died the same day and never wore them. *People are not given the knowledge of their own needs.*

The third question is the one most intriguing to me, because it is at the heart of everything we do. It is *the* question central to every human being: What do people live by?

What brings us meaning? What makes us live a life that matters, instead of one like the demanding rich man in Tolstoy's story, who dies without knowing? The angel discovers the answer.

"I learned that man does not live by care for himself, but by love for others," the angel says, just before he is given his wings back. "When I came to earth as a man, I lived not by care for myself, but by the love that was in the heart of a passerby, and his wife, and because they were kind and merciful to me." Referring to the children left behind by the dying mother whose soul he refused to take, the angel said:

"The orphans lived not by any care they had for themselves; they lived through the love that was in the heart of a stranger.

. . . And all men live, not by reason of any care they have for themselves, but by the love for them that is in other people. . . . It is by love for others that they really live."[2]

In Tolstoy's story, love for others is seen in how people serve others. Love for others is what we are to live by.

Growing up in a religious tradition, I was taught this principle and found it was true for me personally. As an adult who has been in every corner of the world, I have seen that love for others is universal to people of all faiths, as well as those who subscribe to no particular faith. We saw evidence in this in the aftermath of the tsunami that devastated Sri Lanka and Indonesia, as well as in the response to hurricanes Katrina and Rita in the United States.

As a relief worker and a physician, in some of the worst conditions imaginable, I see people helping others who are in need. Usually they are strangers to one another; often they are from different tribes, races, economic or social classes. What draws them together is that someone is in need and someone else is able to provide help.

With that experience in mind, I have come to the following conclusions:

1. Everyone has something to give.

2. Most people are willing to give when they see the need and have the opportunity.

3. Everyone can do something for someone right now.

University scientists who study the brain are discovering that serving others is as much a part of our genetic code as selfinterest is. As a medical doctor, I have seen this firsthand. Kristen Monroe, a professor of political psychology at the University of California–Irvine, says that people act with altruism, a devotion to the welfare of others, when they see their common humanity. I have seen that to be true in the aftermath of hurricanes and wars and epidemics. When we see others as human beings, their needs become real to us, and we respond.

"The dominant mode in social science, evolutionary biology, psychology, and a lot of other fields is to assume that everybody is self-interested," Professor Monroe said. "But that's bad science. Altruism shows you that that isn't true."[3]

Researchers C. Daniel Batson and Nancy Eisenberg of Arizona State University have demonstrated that humans have a tendency toward altruistic behavior.[4] Sociologist Linda Wilson suggests that altruism may be a basic survival instinct. Wilson studied more than a hundred natural disasters and found that victims helping other victims aided each other's recovery. Victims who helped each other tended to avoid some of the psychological problems that would have otherwise been present,

Wilson said.[5]

"The tendency to closely bond with others, acting for the welfare of others as well as oneself, may be deeply rooted in human nature, forged in the remote past as those who bonded together and became part of a group had an increased chance of survival," said Howard Cutler in his book with the Dalai Lama, *The Art of Happiness*. Cutler, a medical doctor, said that studies find people most focused on themselves are more likely to have coronary heart disease, even when other behaviors are controlled.[6] As a physician, I have seen this in my own practice.

After his family was killed in the Holocaust, Samuel Oliner, a sociologist at Humboldt State University, devoted his life to study-ing why people commit acts of violence and why people do good. His interest in why people do good was piqued as he studied rescuers of Jews from the Holocaust, Medal of Honor recipients, hospice volunteers, and rescuers from the 9/11 attacks.

"Without caring, compassion, and love, it is very tough to imagine that the world can come together," he said. "Altruism may be the most potent antidote to a divided world."[7]

Serving others has even been cited as a social necessity. Historian Daniel Boorstin said that colonial and frontier Americans formed groups to do for each other what they couldn't do alone, out of a need for survival. Pilgrims pledged in the Mayflower Compact "to all care of each others good and of the whole by everyone and so mutually."[8] Serving others is written into our country's history. More than two hundred years later, then–Vice President Al Gore said, at a conference on America's future, "Volunteerism is good for the soul, and it's good for the country." Psychiatrist Alfred Adler said that melancholy could be cured in fourteen days if "you try to think every day how you can please someone."[9]

While the scientific evidence shows we are wired toward altruism, there is still a choice involved. The beauty of the choice is that, when we choose to serve others, something wonderful happens.

When I first became a doctor, I knew that I wanted to spend part of each year with people who could not afford proper medical care. This desire came from observing my father. People who had been drinking too much would show up at our house, and my dad would make them something to eat. When he encountered a poor person he always gave them something, usually food or money.

I decided in medical school that I would devote time out of each year to practice medicine where people didn't have adequate medical care. Each year I would pack duffel bags with medicine samples and head to a Third World country. I went for a few weeks to Chernobyl, China, India, and elsewhere by myself.

The seed of service was planted in me by watching my dad. He probably got it from watching his parents. Then it grew while I was in medical school, much like the small plant on the cover of this book.

The seed began to produce an oak tree when I made some off-the-cuff comments at Rotary Club several years ago. The remarks resonated with the audience in a way I could not have anticipated, and the response resulted in my leaving full-time medical practice and starting a global humanitarian agency.

The comments to Rotarians came after I had spent a few weeks in a Cambodian refugee camp, treating as many people as time and supplies allowed. As I sat at a table with local business people, our leader announced that the day's speaker had cancelled at the last minute. "Perhaps Dr. Morsch could tell us about his work in Cambodia."

Walking to the microphone, I had no idea what I was going to say—but I never turn down an opportunity to speak in public about a topic that means so much to me. That day I told the group about the refugees and their horrible conditions. The people in the audience were able to think about the refugees as human beings, not statistics or news stories. I then tossed out a challenge. I didn't know I was going to do it. I wasn't preaching, I was just dreaming out loud.

"Why don't we, who are more prosperous than 98 percent of the rest of the world, find a group or a place or a project to commit to, and do something to help relieve someone's suffering?"

I went back to my table.

"Just tell me when to show up and what I need to bring" was the immediate and overwhelming response.

Within a few weeks we identified a YMCA building in Belize that had been damaged in a hurricane and remained uninhabitable. It had been used as a community center, an educational building, and a public health clinic. Our Rotary chapter took up a collection, and a group of us flew to Belize and repaired the building. It became a place of community service again.

The people there were delighted and grateful. Some of the business people on that trip—men and women who led or had built very successful companies—told me this was the most significant thing they had ever done in their lives. They felt their lives *meant something* while they were doing something for someone else. They had helped someone in a concrete way, and it made them feel alive. They didn't say it made them feel good. Lots of things can do that. This brought them to *life*.

It reminded me of the scene in the movie *City of Joy*, where Patrick Swayze plays the part of a successful surgeon who walks away from money and prestige at a Houston medical center to be a doctor in Calcutta. "I have never felt as *alive* as I feel right now," he declared. This is the human quest.

Philosopher Joseph Campbell said "People say that what we're all seeking is a meaning for life. I don't think that's what we're really seeking. I think that what we're seeking is an experience of being alive, so that our life experiences on the purely physical plane will have resonances within our own innermost being and reality, so that we actually feel the rapture of being alive."[10]

A year after our Belize trip, a group of us flew to Russia to take supplies to a hospital that was running low on nearly everything: needles, gauze, antibiotics, gloves. We could have sent the supplies, but we knew that taking them in person would be better. The response we got from the doctors, nurses, and patients confirmed that. It was one thing to be able to restock the shelves with painkillers and bandages. It was even more significant to the Russians that we cared enough to visit. This face-to-face service made the difference *in them and in us*. We felt that we had made friends for life with these folks who at one time were considered to be the "enemy."

Trips like this motivated me in 1992 to start Heart to Heart International, an organization that seeks out people in need, using mostly volunteers to help meet that need. The global response is always the same. People want to help others. They don't always know how. But they know that, given the opportunity, this is what gives life meaning. It's what we live by.

Pharmaceutical companies now overproduce certain products so that they can donate them to us when we do medical airlifts to regions of natural and economic disaster. Transportation companies factor our airlifts into their routes. The U.S. State Department gives us access to their jumbo cargo planes so we can reach large groups of needy people around the world. Television stations call to ask if they can get the word out. Volunteers line up at the drop of a hat, willing, *wanting* to serve others. Because Heart to Heart uses so many volunteers, we keep overhead costs at 2 percent or less.

I didn't intend to start a humanitarian agency. I was asking the same question as the character in the Tolstoy story: What do we live by? What are we here to do? I discovered what he discovered, that love for others is what we live by, and I wanted to give others the opportunity to do the same.

My dad did small things for people. He showed me that service isn't limited to big dramatic acts. I never saw him rescue someone from a burning building, but I saw him do little things—offer rides, food, money, and time to people—every day. Serving was his lifestyle. It became mine. Who knew that my dad's lifestyle of service would grow into an international agency that gives people the chance to live as he did, only on a global scale?

I still work as a physician, but to accommodate my time with Heart to Heart, I work just a few days a month in small-town emergency rooms. The rest of my time is spent bringing medical products and volunteers together to meet needs throughout the world. I have worked with people who have suffered unfathomable atrocities and been in horrifying places that most folks work hard to avoid. I have seen people serve others in these situations, and witnessed how the action transformed both the person serving and the person being served.

At the end of Dostoevsky's *Brothers Karamazov*, after one of the brothers is convicted of killing his father, another brother burns with fever, and another brother commits suicide. Human corruption, betrayal, and violence become more severe with every page—Alyosha, the youngest brother, meets a group of children who are sad because one of their schoolmates died. Just as it appears that there will be no end to the boys' grief, and no end to the human suffering, and that they are all destined to a life of despair, Alyosha reminds the boys that they showed kindness to the boy who died, and that they should never forget how that felt. He told them to remember: "Yes, there was a moment when I was good and kind and brave."

"You needn't be afraid of life," he continues. "Life is so good when you do something that is good and just."[11]

The philosopher Huston Smith, one of the clearest thinkers I have ever read, said that the greatest power we can have in life is "the power to decide what we want to do with our lives, what we want to give them to."[12]

In this book you will read about the aftermath of the September 11, 2001 terrorist attacks in New York and Washington, DC; about an unspeakable act and a loving response in Kosovo; about the quiet revolution within a Black Panther revolutionary; and about a number of other encounters that reveal the good and just nature that is within each of us. They are stories that come from my experience and observations and that bear witness to the angel's experience in Tolstoy's story: We live by loving and serving others.

The stories in this book point to larger lessons and show people of all ages, income levels, and expertise how to find meaning and significance in their lives, wherever they are. The stories show that serving others is easier and more accessible than you might think. You'll see examples of the way small seedlings sometimes become giant trees.

Through these stories I hope people will be able to see that the world—no matter how small, large, mundane, or terrifying it may appear—needs each of us to participate in it by serving others *with whatever we have at this moment.* Our service doesn't have to change the world. But everyone's world will change as we discover what Tolstoy's angel discovered. We live by loving others. We love others by serving them.

I hope everyone can see the possibility of living this way. Writer Mitch Albom saw it when he began visiting his dying professor, Morrie, and recorded his experiences in the beautiful *Tuesdays with Morrie.* A sports writer, Albom was covering the Wimbledon tennis tournament, surrounded by other selfabsorbed media people and athletes, when he remembered something Morrie told him.

"So many people walk around with a meaningless life," Morrie had said. "They seem half-asleep, even when they're busy doing things they think are important. This is because they're chasing the wrong things. The way you get meaning into your life is to devote yourself to loving others, devote yourself to your community around you, and devote yourself to creating something that gives you purpose and meaning."

Albom considered this amid the crush of the obsessed people at Wimbledon and said, "I knew he was right. Not that I did anything about it."[13]

Why is this such a difficult concept to grasp? Why do some people, like Mitch Albom at that time, recognize that the concept is right, and yet do nothing? Why don't most of us *naturally* live this way of serving others? What are the obstacles to living at a level that is so easily attainable?

Perhaps the primary obstacle is fear of the unknown. We don't know what we might get ourselves into. Things tend to be messier and more complicated than they first appear. We fear that serving others might take us where we lack the emotional energy to go.

Maybe the hesitation comes from an introverted personality. Some people are simply shy, and reaching out to others is extremely uncomfortable and seemingly intrusive. Mother Teresa did it, but she was an extrovert!

Perhaps people don't serve others because they think they lack the time and money. Who has time to look to others' needs when we're running on empty ourselves? And, in a tightening economy, it seems there is little money left over once our obligations are met.

Maybe some don't live in service because they simply don't know what the needs of others are or what they could do—a lack of information.

Perhaps it is a lack of opportunity.

Maybe there is a perceived risk. With Mitch Albom, the risk of getting involved in Morrie's life was that he knew he would be confronted with how self-absorbed and empty his life was.

Perhaps people don't serve others because they may have impure motives—suspecting they are hoping to get something out of it instead of coming from a pure desire to help others.

I think our motives are always going to be mixed.

Robert Coles, a Harvard professor, told Dorothy Day of the Catholic Worker Movement that he had misgivings about his motives for serving others. She said "If we were going to forbid hypocrites to work here with us, there'd be no one to do the work, and no one to do the forbidding!"[14]

But there's at least one other reason why people don't serve others, in my opinion, and I hope this book can change this perception:

People simply don't know how easy this is!

In my years as a physician I have visited thousands of hospital and nursing home rooms. Not once have I seen a patient's room decorated with a trophy, a plaque, a contract, or a bank statement that belonged to the patient. I have never seen a picture of a patient's home or office in one of these rooms. But in almost every room I have seen cards sent by loved ones, pictures drawn by children and grandchildren, expressions of love and hope from the people who matter to them.

We don't have to wait until we are in a hospital room to find out what's really important to us. We can start paying attention now, caring for those around us, and providing hope.

This book does not contain seven steps or seven habits. It isn't a soup for your soul. But it does have lessons—some counterintuitive— to make us seriously consider what we live by. The answers will vary for each of us, but the question is the same.

What do we live by? I trust you will discover some answers for yourself in the following pages. I believe you will see that you can start with something small, something that is in your hands right now. I hope this book will instruct, inspire, and encourage everyone to serve others. That will lead us to something we have been searching for all along.

CHAPTER ONE

GET IN THE BOAT

Be compassionate. And take responsibility
for each other. If we only learned those lessons,
this world would be so much better a place.
Morrie Schwartz[1]

I saw the same images you did: rooftops barely exposed above water, bodies floating in rivers, the Superdome overrun with people and trash, the crush of humanity trying to escape the floods and the shelters. Looters, soldiers, politicians, residents, and journalists reaching their boiling points, often on television.

When I got to New Orleans a few days after Hurricane Katrina blew through in September 2005, telephone poles looked like mangled fingers from an underground monster. Tops of trees were shorn off. Steel beams from unfinished structures bent as if they were still resisting the wind.

I was in an RV with some relief workers, trying to find out where shipments of medicine and mobile medical clinics needed to go. The few other vehicles on the road were either emergency or military, all heavily armed. The only real traffic was in the sky. Hundreds of helicopters ratcheted overhead. There was no electricity. There were no inhabitants. It felt like the end of the world.

On the way to the West Jefferson hospital—one of the three in the Parish that was open—we got lost. Maps were useless because roads were gone. Checkpoint guards made us turn around. As we came over a hill on Veterans Boulevard, we encountered police officers with automatic weapons who waved us down.

We got out, not believing what we saw through the windshield. There was no road ahead. The entire community was under water. Rescue boats were ferrying people from their homes to dry land. The rescuers knew there were still survivors in that water. They would worry about the bodies later, they said.

An elderly woman approached the uniformed men.

"Are you taking people from this neighborhood to see their homes?" she asked.

"No. Maybe in a few weeks. Right now we're trying to get them out, not in."

She turned to me.

"Can you take me to see my house? I want to see what's still there before I leave forever."

Waist-deep in the water was a wiry, unbathed, unshaven Al Pacino–looking man, a cigarette in his mouth and one behind each ear. He was dislodging his fishing boat from a tree branch. "Can you take this lady to see her house?" I shouted to him.

He squinted at her. "What's your address?" She told him.

"We're neighbors. Get in the boat."

She looked at the water. It was a color not found in nature, fouled with floating animals, waste, and debris. Putrid. Toxic. Diseased.

"Wait there," he told her. He slogged out of the water and, like a drenched fireman, carried her to the boat, gently settling her in it. He came back for her 60-year-old niece and plopped her next to her aunt. He looked me over.

"I'm not carrying you. If you want to go, get in."

I waded in, trying to remember the last time I had taken medicine for the hundreds of diseases now soaking through my blue jeans.

What this man was doing was serving his neighbor, as so many others did during this catastrophe. A woman needed a ride. He had a boat.

We motored past (and above!) this lady's church, the school her children attended, and the neighborhood convenience store, which our driver circled for a few minutes, using his landing net to scoop up cartons of cigarettes floating at the rooftop.

"I guess now I'm a looter," he confessed.

He cut the engine a few houses from our destination, and quiet momentum carried us the rest of the way. The bow of the boat gently bumped against the useless gutters of the house. Our companion had lived in this house for seventy-nine years.

"The oak tree looks good," she said, looking at the top third, all that was visible. Who knows what childhood memories that tree held? She gazed at the house for several minutes, the way we visit headstones at cemeteries. No one made a sound.

"The roof's gone," she said, finally.

"Is there something you wish you could get?" I asked her. "I've got my life," she said. "There's nothing in there that

I can't replace."

"We don't want to get stranded here after dark," the driver announced, starting the motor.

On the return trip the propeller stalled briefly after hitting a submerged vehicle.

Walking back up the street, the lady bone dry and I soaking wet, I asked her if she had cried yet.

"None of that has come out," she said. Then she turned to look me right in the eye. "I feel like I died and woke up. That's my old life, out in that water. It's over. Now I have to move on."

The three hurricanes that hit the United States and Central America in 2005—Katrina, Rita, and Wilma—exposed some serious flaws in the way we respond to disaster. I flew into a military base in New Orleans and was hit immediately by the concerns of the local firefighters. They couldn't communicate with other emergency services. They didn't know where the greatest needs were.

I also talked with the directors of emergency operations centers. They told me they could not get through to local, state, or national governments to tell them what they needed. I was approached by a Red Cross worker with a pickup truck loaded with hundreds of boxes of food. "I have all this food, but I don't know where to take it," he said, frustration rising in his voice. "I don't know who needs it."

He gave me dozens of cartons of ready-to-eat meals to give away if I saw anyone who looked hungry. Within a few miles I found an apartment building where people had been stranded since the storm, with no food, water, electricity, or ice. The food was gone in minutes.

The hurricanes exposed flaws in government services, communication systems, levee systems, and in leadership.

But they exposed something else as well.

When people around the world saw the needs of those who were stranded and abandoned, they dropped everything and rushed in. Volunteers were on the scene days before government agencies were deployed. The people who saw the need and showed up were not *organized*. They just showed up.

Caravans of rental trucks loaded with food, water, tents, generators, and other supplies began arriving from states thousands of miles away, paid for by private citizens. Individuals chartered planes to fly people out of the New Orleans Superdome at their own expense and put them in safe lodging. Doctors and nurses arrived, not waiting until they had licensing paperwork approved by the state. Students boarded their college buses and vans and headed south. Neighborhood schools and individuals started fundraisers around the country. Churches and businesses in the affected communities left their doors unlocked to provide shelter for both victims and relief workers.

Some bad things happened there, too. I wish they hadn't. They are a part of human nature that we see more than we care to: shootings, looting, people taking advantage of those who can't defend themselves.

But the other side of human nature, represented by people wanting to help, people having something to give (their time, their resources, their expertise), people acting immediately, showed me that serving others comes as naturally as any of our other behaviors. What I saw in the hurricane aftermath underscored what I said in the Introduction:

- Everyone has something to give.

- Everyone can do something now.

- Many people are willing to give if they are presented the opportunity.

It also revealed something that we don't talk about in our culture very much. There simply are not enough government programs in the world to take care of everyone's needs. There aren't even enough agencies in the United States, the richest country in the world. There aren't enough FEMAs (Federal Emergency Management Administration), there aren't enough National Guards, there aren't enough fire departments or other emergency services, there aren't enough corporations, there aren't enough tax dollars.

There are, however, enough *people*.

We learned from the hurricanes that if we wait for the government—*any* government—we will be waiting too long. Government and Big Business cannot meet every need. They cannot move quickly enough or efficiently enough. In 2005 we saw tens of thousands of people who didn't want to wait. Waiting meant death and suffering for too many people. So they responded and served others. The levees of compassion, love, and service held strong.

Individuals, neighborhoods, and churches responded as if they were made for these kinds of situations, *which is exactly my point!*

When news of hurricane Katrina became known, our offices at Heart to Heart were overwhelmed with calls from individuals. Our staff worked late into the nights and on weekends just to answer the phone calls from people offering to help.

"I'm an EMT [emergency medical technician] and I can help," one caller said. "I have a job interview tomorrow, but forget that. I can change jobs later."

"I can drive supply trucks if you need me," said another. Volunteer drivers showed up in our offices from as far away as San Francisco, just wanting to help. One Californian who showed up had recently returned from the war in Iraq.

One man, who was converting a semi truck into a mobile medical clinic with plans to ship it to a village in Bolivia, called and said he could make it available in New Orleans before sending it to South America.

Costco called. FedEx called. Kmart called. Pharmaceutical companies called. They had something to give. They were willing to serve because they saw the need. They could do something right then; they didn't want to wait.

Institutions can't and won't save us when we need help. And let's admit it: We all need help sometimes. The corollary is that we all need to help sometimes. That's what gives our lives meaning and significance.

We might not all have the opportunity to go to a disaster area. In fact, if too many people come to a disaster area to help, the result can be confusion that compounds the problem. But those who did go can encourage and inspire us to look around our own neighborhoods and become aware of the needs of others. The hurricanes exposed problems that had been invisible or ignored for years. Likewise, there are people within your reach whose needs are not obvious. It doesn't have to take a big event for us to see them. Look around. We can start serving others right where we are.

The test is not what you can do in the aftermath of a hurricane. It's what you can do for the widow next door or the single parent on your street. Does he or she need help running errands? Does your neighbor need someone to read to her? It's not about waiting for disasters to hit. It's about *not* waiting, and serving *now*. It involves an awareness and lifestyle shift that occurs when you simply look at what is within your reach and start where you are.

I am certain that there is someone nearby who you can serve. You and the person in need are neighbors, just like "Al Pacino" and the elderly woman at the edge of their submerged community in New Orleans.

You're looking at the same boat, and the water is rising. It's time to get in.

CHAPTER TWO

GET OVER YOURSELF

If we fail in love, we fail in all things else.
William Sloane Coffin[1]

A stethoscope can put a swagger in any doctor's walk. I don't know that it *always* makes me feel important, but sometimes, I confess, it does. It did during a visit to Mother Teresa's House of Dying Destitutes. The name alone is enough to make you shake your head in dismay. It is in Calcutta, a city that combines population density and intense poverty. Add extreme heat and a desperate lack of sanitation, and, well, you get the picture. The House of Dying Destitutes is run by the Sisters of Charity, a Catholic order founded by Mother Teresa. It is the place people are brought when it is clear they are going to die, but they have no one to care for them and no money to pay for someone to care for them. So the people there are truly the poorest of the poor.

I had met Mother Teresa years ago when I was traveling through India, at least ten years before Heart to Heart was started. I witnessed the compassion she and the others had for poor people and vowed that I would return to work alongside her in some way. In fact, I told her that I would come back with medicine to help ease the pain of these people. Maybe the medicine could save some lives, I told her. She smiled, thanked me, and shook my hand. She pointed to a box of outdated medicines that someone had collected and sent.

"We have some medicine," she said.

"I'll bring more than that," I told her. "And it won't be American discards, either."

It was several years later when I did return, this time with 90 volunteers and 50 tons of medicine worth more than $12 million. All of it was donated by pharmaceutical companies. None of it was outdated. It was specifically for use in Calcutta. I could tell Mother Teresa was pleased.

But we didn't want to just deliver medicine and leave. We wanted to work alongside the Sisters and make a difference in people's lives. As I look back on it, some of us were a bit full of ourselves. We had arrived to Do Good.

Our group divided into work teams to visit various sites throughout the city. My small team went to the House of Dying Destitutes with a big idea. We were going to Relieve Suffering! This was the location where Mother Teresa's work had begun. It started when she, a young Albanian missionary, encountered a woman dying in the street. The woman was covered with insects. Rats didn't wait for the woman to die before they started in. People passing in the streets simply hurried around the body, as if it were trash that someone had neglected to clean up.

Appalled, this newly called Sister picked up the woman and carried her to a local hospital. The medical staff refused to treat the woman because she was unable to pay. But Mother Teresa demanded treatment for her and refused to leave the hospital. When she promised to make a scene the medical staff relented. This experience led to Mother Teresa's getting city officials to donate a facility where people could bring those who were dying with the assurance that the dying would be properly cared for during their last days. Thousands have come there, or been left on the doorstep, since the House opened in the 1940s.

What galled me as a physician was that many of these people died, and are dying, of treatable diseases. Dysentery is one of the main causes of death there. It is a very treatable condition, with the right medicine and clean water. Other people were dying from diseases that have been eradicated elsewhere.

So, with all of my medical knowledge and certainty, I arrived at the House of Dying Destitutes. I had something to offer,I thought. It is just the kind of place where a doctor should be assigned. I wanted to put this place out of business. With great optimism, I looked at the sign outside the building and thought "Soon I will change that sign and this facility will be called 'The House of Hope for the Living.'" I knew I would make a difference.

Sister Priscilla graciously greeted our group and assigned us to various tasks. When she turned to me, I introduced myself as a physician from the United States. I put my stethoscope around my neck. I knew this was a place where little or no medical care was available to these "untouchables." What we had to offer was miraculous. My mind began to review my medical training. This was a place that needed me.

"Follow me, please," directed Sister Priscilla with her soft British accent. We entered the men's ward—a large, open room with rows of cots cradling what I can only describe as skeletons with skin on them. Some were tossing in pain, too weak to fight their afflictions or even to eat. To my surprise, we proceeded quickly through this ward and on to the next. This was the women's ward. It was a similar room filled with emaciated women whose vacant eyes stared, unseeing. But again we passed through this room without stopping.

"Can there be a needier place than this?" I wondered, my mind reviewing the more serious diseases I might encounter.

We entered a primitive kitchen where a simple lunch of rice was being prepared over an open fire. "How odd," I thought. "Why would they want a doctor in a kitchen?" But Sister Priscilla led me through the kitchen, out the back door, and into a narrow alley. What were they going to have me do? Were there people waiting outside who were too sick to come into the House?

Sister Priscilla pointed to a very large pile of garbage. It smelled revolting.

"We need you to take this garbage down the street to the dump," she explained, handing me two buckets and a shovel. "The dump is several blocks down the street on the right. You can't miss it." With a nod and a slight smile she was gone.

In the United States we dispose of food scraps neatly in the disposal attached to our kitchen sinks. Paper and plastic are put in garbage cans. Much of what we discard goes in tidy recycling bins. Not so in Calcutta. Every bit of paper and plastic is reused several times. Nothing goes to waste. The huge pile before me was of stinking, rotting, putrefying food garbage—only the stuff that can't be used again.

Recovering from a momentary stunned silence, I began to react. Garbage? Don't they get it? I am a doctor! I felt like quoting the Bones McCoy character in the old television show *Star Trek:* "Dammit Priscilla, I'm a doctor, not a garbage man!"

Instead, I put my stethoscope in my pocket and attacked the pile. I filled the buckets and headed down the street. It seemed that every pair of eyes on the crowded street looked at me as I carried my fetid burden through the humid morning air. I slung the contents onto the dump and went back for the next load, trying not to notice that people emerged from the shadows of the dump to forage through what I had just added.

I began feeling sorry for myself. I had come expecting to do something meaningful. Did they have no sense of stewardship? Anyone could have carried the garbage. I could have been in the building, saving lives! If anyone could appreciate the educated class, it should be the people of India!

It was mid-afternoon when I finished. Sweating profusely, smelling like the heap itself, I set down the buckets and shovel and headed back through kitchen, the women's ward, and the men's ward—places where my gifts could have been used—prepared to

rejoin my team and say goodbye to Sister Priscilla for the day. Just
before she appeared, I saw it: a small, hand-lettered sign that read, in
Mother Teresa's own words, "We can do no great things, only small
things with great love."

My heart melted. I had completely missed the point. I
needed this lesson. Serving others is not about how much I know,
how many degrees I've earned, or what my credentials are. It is
about attitude and availability to do whatever is needed—with love.
Mother Teresa had pierced the armor I worked so long to construct.
She removed the armor around my heart, through Sister Priscilla.

My friendship with Mother Teresa blossomed after that. I
understood her life and purpose better, and that made me want
to work with her in as many ways as possible. I wanted to provide
the opportunity for others to see that shoveling garbage can be
transforming.

Perhaps the most amazing (and amusing!) manifestation of my
friendship came about when she was visiting Vietnam, serving the
poor in the northern part of that country. An attorney from Kansas
City was in Hanoi at the time, still wrestling with demons from his
tour as an American soldier. On a busy street, this attorney thought
he recognized Mother Teresa. He had never met her before, or even
seen her in public. But, since her appearance was unmistakable, he
was confident. So he crossed the street and introduced himself. She
was her usual gracious self, and then asked him a few questions. He
told her he was an American. She asked from where. He said Kansas
City. She said, "Oh, have you heard of Heart to Heart?"

She told him about the work we had done in Calcutta. Intrigued,
he phoned me when he got back to the States. Over lunch I told him
I wanted to provide medicines and supplies to the poverty-stricken
areas of Vietnam. Soon the first U.S. aircraft flew into Vietnam so we
could assist people in hospitals, leper colonies, and refugee camps,
and it was covered by the major news media from around the world.

As I trace the dots backward, much of my medical service to others arose from the transformative experience of shoveling the refuse of dying people. Before that, shoveling garbage in the sweltering stench of Calcutta would have been beneath me. My gifts, training, and talent were invested for other, more lofty tasks, I assumed. I had the stethoscope to prove it! The sign on Mother Teresa's wall was a reality check for me. I wanted to do great things. I learned that shoveling garbage with love is different from just shoveling garbage.

"Love should come before logic," Alyosha Karamazov tells his brother Ivan. "Only then will man be able to understand the meaning of life."[2] Logic was telling me that my gifts would best be used in the wards with the patients. But Sister Priscilla, taught by Mother Teresa, knew better. She knew that something else needed to happen first. I needed to start with love—in the garbage pile.

Service to others, as I understand it now, often starts with what seems insignificant, maybe even unpleasant. It was the lesson Jesus taught his followers when, near the end of his life, he wrapped a towel around himself, took up a basin of water, and washed the feet of his disciples.[3] This act took a strong stomach and an enlightened sense of what is real. It starts here at the very bottom, his action said, at the point where the grime of the world meets you, that's where love begins. I don't know if you have ever gotten close to other people's feet. As a doctor, I assure you it can be a challenge.

It is one of life's great mysteries that, for us to experience love, purpose, and meaning, we must begin at the place where we find ourselves most resistant. What was Sister Priscilla trying to tell me? That what I offer suffering people has to be consciously based in love, or my actions won't matter.

It made me think of the line I read in Jim Wallis' book *God's Politics*: "Nobody gets to heaven without a letter of reference from the poor."[4]

I have brought groups of volunteers back to Calcutta several times. Often the volunteers come with the same kind of certainty, full of themselves, as I was. But every one of them is transformed in the act of serving others.

One of our volunteers fed fish and rice to a man at the House of the Dying Destitutes who was too weak to feed himself. Part way through the feeding, the man became agitated and clutched his throat, mouth open. Fortunately, our volunteer was able to reach into the man's mouth and remove a fishbone caught in the man's throat.

The man fearfully shook his head when offered another spoonful of rice and fish. Wondering what to do, our volunteer noticed another man motioning to him. He was offering his two tangerine slices; they would feel soothing on a damaged throat. One dying man offered aid to another dying man.

"I will never, ever again say that I have nothing to give someone in need," said the volunteer.

People who had encounters like mine were changed by their experiences. Laying aside their education and their professional qualifications, they simply helped people who couldn't help themselves. Some returned to their own communities and began volunteering in clinics and missions. My daughter, who had come with me on a Heart to Heart airlift to Calcutta, organized the college women in her dormitory to work in Calcutta during their spring break.

The volunteers who have gone on these airlifts to Calcutta and elsewhere tell me they look at their everyday world differently afterward. Some volunteer at rescue missions or food banks or medical or legal clinics. Some just see their colleagues differently. Looking for ways to serve others becomes a daily practice. It gives meaning to their day. I see a transformation in people every time we do an airlift to some needy area.

Volunteers don't at first know how to respond to the needs they see. Once they assist someone who lives an ocean away, they see the needs in their own neighborhoods. I have often seen it happen that a person has to leave his country in order to truly see his own community and its needs.

In his book *Adam,* Henri Nouwen tells of a New York socialite who, despite her marriages to successful businessmen, her wealth, fame, children and social status, was suicidal. She came to visit Nouwen for spiritual guidance because he was a well-known religious scholar, writer, and priest. He had left his prestigious academic positions at both Yale and Harvard divinity schools to work in a home for disabled adults. He immediately put his visitor to work feeding one of the people who could not feed himself.

In the years following the woman's visit, she told Nouwen that "Something quite profound happened on my visit. . . . I am no longer as depressed as I was before, because I feel more connected with myself."[5] It seems contradictory that, in order for us to understand ourselves and connect with our true selves, we must go outside of ourselves and serve the needs of others. But I am convinced this is the way it works.

I know that my job as a physician is to help people feel better. They pay me to do that. But I also know that my true vocation lies somewhere beyond getting paid for my services. Who am I, apart from being a doctor? I see the answer most clearly when I work in a refugee camp in Thailand, or organize a bike hike for my son's Boy Scout troop. That is when I feel most alive. When I get outside myself, my cultural role, as I was forced to do at the House of Dying Destitutes, I see life more clearly. Sometimes my true vocation lies in putting away the stethoscope—the badge that tells the world who I am, or at least who I think I am—and picking up a shovel at a garbage pile in Calcutta.

It feels counterintuitive at first, but the sign on the wall tells us that this is the beginning: Do small things with love. When any of us drop the cultural symbols of who we are, we open ourselves to acts of service that others need. People in our families, our neighborhoods, and our communities need servants, not role players who know themselves only as doctors, teachers, military personnel, mothers, fathers, or business leaders.

There are some similarities between Mother Teresa and Henri Nouwen. Both set aside their self-interest to serve others. What I am most attracted to is their passion. Serving others gave purpose to their days. It became their life. I have seen people break their addiction to materialism, individualism, and sensationalism when they began serving others. Serving makes us see ourselves as part of a larger picture.

Regarding the disabled young man for whom he was responsible, Nouwen said that Adam's teaching was that compassion, not competition, is the way to fulfill our human vocation.[6] This was the lesson of the local Rotary Club in my town when we started looking for places where we could serve—first in a hurricane-damaged YMCA in Belize, then in an undersupplied hospital in Russia, and now throughout the world. We discovered that Rotary could be more than a social and business networking club. It could be, and did become, an organization living out its true vocation.

I have often wondered why we don't see that we are here to serve others—especially when it is so gratifying to do so. A friend in San Diego, Gail Shingler, said she had failed to see herself as someone who has something to offer others simply because she lacked confidence.

"I felt that I needed some kind of training before I started doing things for people other than members of my family," Gail said. "Whenever I heard people talk about serving others I felt as if my heart wanted to do the same, but I didn't know how. I couldn't move to another country or anything drastic. But I felt that I needed some training or equipping even for doing something right where I was."

Sitting in church one morning she sensed that the time had come for her to stop thinking about it and start doing something. She talked to her husband and a close friend. The friend called her a few days later.

"She said that she had awakened in the middle of the night with the thought of where I should go," Gail said. "She woke up with three words very clearly: Ronald McDonald House."

The McDonald's restaurant corporation provides houses near hospitals where families can stay when their children are being treated for cancer and other serious diseases. Gail's friend had been to a local Ronald McDonald House with her Brownie troop, and noticed that the staff always had too much to do and the house always needed cleaning. Gail called the house near San Diego's Children's Hospital and the director invited her over.

"The director just seemed so tired," Gail said. "I told her I could commit to two hours a week, and would do whatever she needed."

Now, on Sunday mornings, Gail vacuums, washes walls, and wipes down high chairs.

"The house gets a lot of use, unfortunately, so it's pretty dirty," she said. "But given the reason people are there, I felt they deserved better."

After her first day of cleaning, she said she wasn't tired. "My body was excited," she said. "I felt that this was what

I was meant to do."

Keep in mind, Gail has three children under the age of ten, and is a talented artist and a certified educator. The best part of her week, she said, is those two hours on Sunday morning. Why?

"We're here to do chores," she said. "When I'm driving to Ronald McDonald House, I don't fret about what my husband thinks of me or what my kids think of me. I only think about what God thinks of me."

Commenting on getting the idea of going to Ronald McDonald House from her friend, Gail said it showed how interconnected we all are.

"It's all a web," she said. "You can walk through a web and be surprised by it and have it freak you out. Or, you can walk up to it, step back, and say 'Oh my!'"

When Mother Teresa died I was sad but also grateful for the lessons she and the other Sisters of Charity taught me. My admiration for her connected me to a little village in Kosovo a few years ago, when I was working in a military hospital with my Army Reserve unit. I was stationed at Camp Bondsteel, not far from where Mother Teresa lived when she received her call to serve the poor. She was Albanian, just like the people we were in Kosovo to protect. I visited the statue of her in downtown Skopje, Macedonia, where she spent her childhood years.

I spent considerable time gazing at the memorial in the middle of a Skopje street and at the house where she had lived. They reminded me of the sign that pierced my self-centeredness: "We can do no great things, only small things with great love." Though it made me uncomfortable at first, my discomfort soon gave way to gratitude.

I got into a conversation about Mother Teresa with one of the military chaplains at Camp Bondsteel, and he told me that she visited the area several times while she was growing up. She was born in Kosovo, and her family moved to Skopje. There is a village nearby with a chapel that has a Black Madonna icon. Mother Teresa and her family traveled to this chapel from Skopje every year to visit the special shrine. Before the Serb/Albanian war, more than 150,000 people made a pilgrimage to this chapel each year. It was in this chapel that Mother Teresa received her call to become a nun and serve the poor. It was where the roots of doing small things with love began to grow.

Naturally, I wanted to go to this chapel but, as a soldier, I couldn't just organize a convoy to go sightseeing! As it turned out, several things came together one Christmas night that allowed me to go. I attended the Protestant candlelight service with one of the colonels from the base. At the end of the service I asked if he wanted to join me for the midnight Mass in the same chapel. He said he was going with some of the soldiers to a Mass in another town, but I was welcome to go along. I asked where they were going, and couldn't believe my ears.

A Special Forces team had organized a convoy to take a small group of officers to Letnecia, the town with the chapel where Mother Teresa discovered her true vocation. The officer asked me if I would like to go with them. If so, they were leaving in thirty minutes.

I rushed back to the hospital to get my helmet, flak vest, and weapon, and joined the convoy. Six Humvees made their way up narrow, winding roads into the mountains. Radios crackled and security was tight. About a mile from the village I could see the blazing lights of what is now a beautiful cathedral. We drove up to it, parked our vehicles and climbed the icy stairs, dressed in full battle gear, our M-16s slung over our shoulders and pistols in holsters around our waists. I don't know what the local people thought, but they seated us in the first several rows, right under the beautiful Black Madonna shrine.

The service started at 11 and ended at about 12:30 in the morning. The priest arranged for some of the soldiers to participate in the Mass by reading the scriptures. I have been to a lot of religious services around the world—country churches, great cathedrals, synagogues, and mosques—but I had never before seen armed soldiers standing next to the religious leader, participating in worship!

In his sermon, the priest said how thankful the people of his village were that the killing had stopped for the time being.

After the Mass they had a children's program where kids sang, recited poetry, and reenacted the nativity scene—just as we had at home!

Afterward, the priest invited us to the rectory for cookies and coffee. I asked him about Mother Teresa's childhood visits to the church. He told us that, even after the family moved to Skopje, they traveled across the mountains each year to visit this site during a religious festival. On one of those visits, when she was 18, Agnes (her name before she adopted Mother Teresa) sensed God calling her into service. When I told the priest of my connection to her, he seemed very excited. He rushed out of the room to his study and brought back a picture of her, insisting that I keep it. Having had a wonderful time in Letnecia, our unusual convoy returned to the military base at around three in the morning.

As I reflect on that little village in war-torn Kosovo, I marvel that it was the site where a little girl was born who would become one of the most beloved women in history. In his book *Great Souls*, David Aikman, a former senior editor for *Time* magazine, calls her a person who changed the twentieth century. She changed the world, won a Nobel Prize, and inspired millions of people, including me, to look at service as a way to find meaning for our lives.

Every one of us is confronted with the option of picking up our stethoscopes (or diplomas or titles or uniforms) or picking up a shovel and doing something small, with love, for someone else. Both have value. Mother Teresa's example helped me want to create opportunities for others, like for my own daughter, to experience the deeper vocation to which I believe we are all called, that of serving others. An encounter with dying destitutes, for many of us, removed blinders from our eyes and allowed us to see opportunities for service throughout our everyday lives.

What tenets did Mother Teresa live by? What did her life teach us?

She taught me to do small things for others. With love. I hope that is what my life teaches others. I hope that's what Heart to Heart communicates.

It doesn't always have to start with a trash heap. It starts with whatever is within reach.

CHAPTER THREE

LOOK IN YOUR HAND

If you don't let me serve you, I'll die.
Madame Babette Hersant[1]

When I joined the Army Reserves in 1993, I didn't do it because I was pro-war, or because I thought that waging war was noble. I joined the Reserves because of the opportunity I had as a doctor to ease the suffering that war causes. As an Army doctor, I care not only for our soldiers but also for civilians caught in the crossfire, as well as for those we call "the enemy."

In 2000 I was deployed to Kosovo, after NATO bombings brought the hostilities between the Albanians and the Serbs to a standstill. My unit first went to Fort Benning, Georgia, where we were trained in matters such as laws of war, clearing an area of land mines, weapon proficiency, and the historical roots of the Balkans conflicts. We were assigned battle gear, complete with flak vests and Kevlar helmets. Then we were shipped off to Kosovo.

I worked in the mobile hospital at Camp Bondsteel, a seven-square-mile sprawling complex of tents, permanent structures, fences, and every imaginable type of military vehicle. The camp accommodated ten thousand soldiers. Helicopters constantly took off and landed. Every few hundred yards there were towers from which heavily armed lookouts scanned the woods and roads surrounding the camp. Camp Bondsteel was a selfcontained city. It provided its own water, sewage, and sanitation, fire and police, laundry, food and hospital services, and even jail. There was a chapel, a movie theater, a store, a library, a barbershop (all hair styles were the same—short!) and a coffee bar.

Everyone inside the camp was heavily armed. Even as you walked from sleeping quarters to the mess tent, you carried a gun. The doctors carried smaller weapons so we could keep our hands free to take care of patients. It was a strange feeling examining a patient in the emergency room with a pistol on my right hip and an ammo pouch on the left.

What seemed even stranger about all of the security was that much of what went on inside the camp was recreation— ping pong, volleyball, basketball, workout gyms, movie theaters, television lounges, as well as a Burger King and other amenities. It looked like a heavily armed summer camp.

Still, there was always a threat that lingering hostilities between the Serbs and Albanians would boil over and someone might attack. As part of the NATO forces in the area, Americans were there to maintain the fragile peace agreement between recently warring groups. NATO bombs were no longer falling while I was there. Only emotional ones.

When I first arrived with my unit, the medical staff showed me to the barracks, where I met my roommates, two dentists and a combat psychiatrist. Our housing was a large tent with a wooden floor. Soon after I set my pack on my bed, I was taken to the hospital to see where I would be spending the winter. The hospital was more modern than some of the country hospitals in Kansas where I work as an emergency room doctor!

The x-ray units, surgical areas, and MRI equipment were state-of-the-art. Most of the patients at Bondsteel did not have war-related injuries, I was told. While there were still some unexploded land mines in the area that accidentally injured civilians, most of our patients were soldiers who twisted ankles playing basketball, or people from outside the camp who had suffered a car accident, burn, or shooting. We set bones, delivered babies, performed tonsillectomies—in general, acted like a small-town hospital.

Within just a few hours of arriving in Kosovo I was shown the mess tent, and sat down for my first meal. I was tired and hungry from the long trip.

Soon after I began eating, a professional-looking Albanian woman entered the mess hall and walked to my table.

"Are you Dr. Morsch?" she asked. "Yes. How can I help you?"

"I'm Drita Perezic, General Sanchez's translator. We have been looking forward to your being here," she said in perfect English. "General Sanchez would like to ask you a favor."

Word had gotten to the general that the head of a humanitarian group had been assigned to Camp Bondsteel, and before I arrived he had checked out Heart to Heart. And me.

Drita told me one of the most heartbreaking stories I have ever heard. Earlier that year, Merita Shabiu, an 11-year-old Albanian girl, was abducted, raped, and killed by an American soldier based at Camp Bondsteel. That soldier and his driver then buried Merita's body in a snow bank outside the nearby town of Vitina. All of this happened on the first day General Sanchez had taken command of Bondsteel.

I remember shaking my head the whole time Drita talked to me. I had a vague recollection of reading about this back in the United States. As Drita talked, I kept wondering to myself: Why is she telling me this? Merita is dead. The soldier has already confessed and is in a military prison for the rest of his life at Fort Leavenworth. What can I do? It doesn't sound as if they need a doctor.

"There isn't much else the military can do for Merita's family, but they aren't doing very well," Drita concluded. "They're still full of grief for their daughter. The father showed up at one of our checkpoints recently and said they were out of food and that he was sick."

"If he's sick, then bring him in to the hospital and any one of us can check him out," I said. "Bring him to a doctor."

She hesitated.

"He doesn't really need a doctor as much as he needs someone to reach out to him. He's hurting in a way that the military can't help."

Her next question wasn't a great philosophical inquiry. She didn't want to know why bad things happen to good people. She didn't wonder where God was in this tragedy.

"Do you think you can do something for this family?" she asked.

I had no idea what I could do, but I said yes.

Within a few days our convoy of four Humvees carrying ten soldiers in full battle gear headed out of Camp Bondsteel and into the mountains that separate Kosovo from Macedonia. The Shabiu family lives in those mountains in a small village of just a few houses. Once we left the pavement of the city we drove for two hours on a steep and narrow road that seemed more suited for herds than our wide vehicles. Trees were so close to the path that they knocked the side mirrors off the vehicles. The lead driver nearly tipped his Humvee over.

The family has no phone or electricity, so there was no way of telling them that a military unit was on its way. I can't imagine the fear they must have felt when we pulled up to their tiny house. The soldiers set up watch around the perimeter of the house as if it were a military action. One could never be too careful.

Hamdi Shabiu, Merita's father, and Remzije, her mother, cautiously stepped out of their house, their other four children hiding behind them. After what had happened to Merita, the sight of American soldiers must have been alarming. I introduced myself through a translator. Hamdi and Remzije soon began scurrying around their property, looking for something for us all to sit on. They looked for cups so they could serve us tea. I was moved by their hospitality, especially in light of the fact that an American soldier had caused their heartbreak. Now they were surrounded by soldiers, and they wanted to make us feel at home.

Judging by the parents' actions, they had no enemies, despite what had happened. Inside his home, I told Hamdi that I was there not as a soldier (despite my uniform) but as a friend, and that I wanted to check up on him and his family. I gave each of them a physical examination and some medicines.

"Tell me about Merita," I said to Hamdi.

He looked up at the wall for a moment, and his eyes filled with tears. I followed his gaze, and my eyes filled as well. Still hanging on the wall was Merita's backpack and pink coat, as if she were going to walk in soon and put them on, ready for another day of school.

"Merita was a beautiful little girl who was very happy," he began. "When the NATO jets flew over our village on their way to bomb Serbian positions, Merita would go out to the top of the hill and wave to them. She knew they were coming to rescue us."

The Shabius had been forced to move to Vitina during the war. Just a few days before the NATO strikes began, Hamdi and Remzije were taken by Serb police and beaten severely—simply because they were Albanian, they said. Hamdi's injuries were so bad that blood came out of his ears. Then they were taken outside the city and dumped in the forest.

"Our children had no idea where we were, so they were very frightened," he said. But the arrival of the NATO jets gave the Shabiu family a sense that their world would be safe soon. Merita, in particular, was happy because the jets meant that she could go back to school and someday become a doctor.

But one day Merita did not come home from school. Her mother, father, brothers, and sister searched for her without success. Finally, Hamdi reported her disappearance to the local police.

Two days later, children in a schoolyard told Hamdi that there was a child's body in a nearby building. They pointed to a bombed-out structure surrounded by U.S. soldiers. He identified himself to the soldiers and told them that his daughter was missing.

"They took me into the building, and I saw a U.S. officer crying," Hamdi said. The officer showed Hamdi a photo and asked if it were Merita.

"She died a horrible death," Hamdi said. "I almost passed out when I saw her."

The photo showed his beautiful daughter with beaten, swollen eyes, bruises around her neck, and what appeared to be a bullet hole in her forehead. Her thin, yellow hair was matted behind her head. Hamdi showed me photos of Merita when she was healthy and happy. Then he showed me the photos of her after her body was found. I cried as if she were my own daughter.

We talked about Merita a while longer, and I asked if I could see where she was buried. They took me to a small community cemetery, where graves were marked only by a few sticks and an empty cup, an Albania custom I did not understand. Hamdi pointed out which grave was Merita's. The dirt walls were already caving in. Animals had evidently been digging there.

"Doesn't she have a headstone?" I asked.

"I am a woodcutter and a beekeeper, and we're in a war. How would I pay for a headstone?" he said.

As we went back to his house, my mind was racing. I was angered and disgusted by what the soldier had done. I was also frustrated. We can't bring this daughter back. We can't change the economy of this village in Kosovo. We can't make hostile parties like each other. What can we offer someone in a situation like this?

I felt completely inadequate. What small thing, in love, would be meaningful to this family in pain? I couldn't undo the awful thing that had been done to their daughter. I looked sadly at Merita's pink coat. I could not do *nothing*.

A statement by the writer Frederick Buechner came to mind: "True peace, the high and abiding peace that passeth all understanding, is to be had not in retreat from the battle, but only in the thick of the battle."[2]

I went to the Humvee, got my laptop computer out of my pack, and went back into the Shabiu's home. They watched me turn it on, then open a program that had software for creating art. With the computer's mouse, I began to draw a headstone.

"What would you like Merita's headstone to say?" I asked. Hamdi and Remzije looked at each other and talked quietly as it slowly dawned on them what I was doing.

"You're going to make a headstone on the computer?" they asked.

"I'm going to design it, with your help, and then someone else will build it." I was just talking off the top of my head, making it up as I went along. Something had to be done for this grieving family. Something had to bring dignity to Merita.

Looking at the other soldiers, I signaled that I had no idea what we were going to do. But the soldiers and our translator were smiling. They knew we were embarking on an important journey with this family.

Soon everyone—mom, dad, and kids—was excitedly talking about what should be on the marker to honor Merita. It should have an Albanian flag, they said. Hamdi said it should also have an American flag. I stopped drawing for a moment and looked at him. "Wasn't it an American who killed your daughter?" I asked.

"I am not an educated man," he said. "But I know that this soldier was not following orders when he killed my daughter. I will not blame all Americans or all American soldiers."

I pasted in the flags and put them in the upper corners of the headstone. I wrote Merita's name prominently in the middle, with the dates of her life on earth.

"Anything else?" I asked. "Something you want to say about her?"

More discussion between mom and dad. "Write this: 'She taught us to love one another,'" her father said.

We still had room, so I asked if they wanted a picture of her engraved into the marker. They handed me a photo that brought me to tears again. She looked like an angel. I thought about my own kids and wondered how a parent could bear the death of a child—especially such a brutal death.

I set the photo on a table and took a picture of it with my digital camera. Then I loaded the image into the computer and pasted it into the headstone. Finally, on my computer screen, we had a tribute to Merita. The family couldn't believe it. I told them we would return with a headstone and give Merita a proper burial.

How we would produce that headstone was a complete mystery to me. But my experience told me that someone wanted to help but just didn't know how. I decided to trust the process, get the word out, and watch people respond.

The reason so many people don't help each other is that they don't know how—they are paralyzed by their lack of information. Yet at their core they *want* to help, and they know that they should. They know that their lives will mean more as they serve others. They just need some handles.

It didn't take long for word about our visit to the Shabiu family to circulate among the soldiers at Bondsteel and other American outposts throughout Kosovo. Within days, officers stopped me wherever I was and handed me wads of cash donated by their units. Officers came to me in tears, saying "Thank you for giving us a chance to tell them how we feel."

Most of the soldiers had not met any of the Shabiu family. They only knew that something terrible had happened to them, and that there was an opportunity to reach out to them through this headstone. Within days of my first meeting with the Shabius, American soldiers had donated more than $4,000 to help relieve their suffering.

We found an engraver who would make the monument for Merita and, to be certain everything the Shabius wanted would be on the headstone, we made another unannounced visit. It happened that our visit fell on a day when, traditionally, Muslim families have a great feast to celebrate the end of Ramadan—which we didn't realize until we arrived.

Bringing out festive cakes and pastries to welcome us, the Shabius confided that they had planned to go to another village for the day. But, although Hamdi pleaded with them, the children refused to go, saying that they "had a feeling" that the American soldiers were coming to visit them. They were actually waiting outdoors for us, watching for our convoy to come around the bend of the narrow mountain road. When we arrived, Hamdi said God had brought us together on this very special Muslim holiday.

A few days later we took the money collected from the soldiers and opened a bank account in the nearby town. I wish I had videotaped that event. Several U.S. soldiers, dressed in camouflage, helmets, and boots, and all heavily armed, arrived at the bank, setting off every alarm. I stepped up to the counter and told the wide-eyed teller "I want to open an account." She looked at me, then at all the soldiers who had filled the small bank, and could only nod. The rest of the customers evacuated the building when we arrived, just like they did in old movies of when the gunslinger and his gang entered a saloon!

The deposit was considerably more than the cost of the headstone, so I included a stipulation that the money could only be withdrawn if it were going to be used for humanitarian purposes, and made the Army chaplain a co-signer. The Army had allowed me to continue some humanitarian efforts while I was there, permitting the shipment of clothes, medicines, and eyeglasses to the base. Volunteers then distributed them to people in need.

Lions Clubs in Indiana had collected 3,000 pairs of eyeglasses for the people of Kosovo, and the Bondsteel optometrist was organizing ways to get them to the neediest people in the province. I knew some of the money in this account would help cover those expenses. Children at Black Bob Elementary School in Olathe, Kansas, had collected and packed twenty-two large boxes of children's winter coats, gloves, and hats for the people in the area. I knew this fund would help cover shipping costs, too.

A few weeks later we headed into the mountains again, this time with a truck carrying Merita's headstone. I couldn't wait for the Shabius to see it. When we arrived, they greeted us as if we were family. We had brought them hope on our first visit, and that made us brothers and sisters. They wept when they saw the headstone. The image of Merita, smiling her beautiful smile, etched into the granite, brought out emotions in her parents that I hope I never have to experience.

Hamdi and Remzije hugged me for a very long time. Merita had begun to feel like my own daughter. Anne Lamott said "It is only by experiencing that ocean of sadness in a naked and immediate way that we come to be healed."[3] This was both sad and healing.

Merita was re-buried in a community cemetery, her headstone prominent among the others. Nearby was a sacred site, the mass grave of Albanian soldiers who had died in a military action against the Serbs. Far from being forgotten, she was now in a place of dignity, her grave marked with a stone that rose up out of the ground like a sunflower.

Several religious traditions were represented as we conducted a brief service at the new site. The differences didn't matter. Grief, combined with hope, blurred all the lines to produce one shared experience—gratitude.

"What is experienced as most unique often proves to be most solidly embedded in the common condition of being human," wrote Henri Nouwen.[4] This was unique and unforgettable.

What Merita and her family experienced is beyond comprehension. And yet, through the headstone, we were able to share our humanity and serve one another. We are called to exercise hospitality to each person we encounter. "The term *hospitality* should not be limited to its literal sense of receiving a stranger in our house,"

Nouwen wrote, "but as a fundamental attitude toward our fellow human being, which can be expressed in a great variety of ways."[5] In this case, it was expressed by the simple act of providing a headstone for a girl who should not have died.

How did I know that reaching for my computer was what they needed at the time? I didn't. What I learned was the lesson Moses learned while he was tending sheep. In the Old Testament book of Exodus, God talks to Moses through a burning bush. God tells Moses to go to the Pharaoh and demand that the slaves of Israel be set free. My free translation of the dialogue goes like this:

Moses: "You can't be serious. I have a speech impediment."

God: "I am serious. You can do it."

Moses: "Pharaoh won't believe me."

God: "Tell him I sent you."

Moses: "Then he *really* won't believe me. I can't do it."

God: "What do you have in your hand?"

Moses: "A staff for herding sheep."

God: "Throw it on the ground, then pick it up again."

On the ground the staff becomes a serpent, but it changes back into a staff when Moses picks it up. I think God is telling Moses that whatever he has at hand will be enough to do the job.

I had a laptop computer. Soldiers throughout Kosovo had dollar bills in their hands. That was enough to bring honor to Merita and dignity to her family. In the previous chapter I mentioned the dying man who offered his few slices of tangerine to soothe the throat of another dying man. What he had in his hand was just what the other man needed. *This is always the case.* For whatever reason, we feel that we need more training, more education, more skills assessments, more time, or more money. We don't. *We are the answers to others' prayers.*

It is sometimes hard to see ourselves as an answer to prayer. Instead of waiting until we're able to organize a large effort to help people, we can start where we are, with what we have. I spoke on the topic of serving others to a group in Glasgow, Scotland, and a man approached me afterward in frustration. His community needed to build a home for unmarried mothers to have their babies. There was no adequate facility in the region and he believed that he had the skills to build one.

"Congratulations," I said. "I wish you the best in this very important venture."

"You don't understand," he said. "I want to build it, but there is so much government red tape involved that we haven't even begun. I'm very frustrated by the way the government is keeping this great idea from happening."

"How long have you been trying to get this done?" I asked.

"More than two years," he said, with exasperation in his voice.

"And in those two years how many women have you helped?" I said.

"None!" he exclaimed. "The government won't let me!"

"I have a suggestion," I said. "Do you have a house?"

"Yes."

"Does it have a spare room?"

"Yes."

"Then open that spare room to someone who needs it right now. Don't wait until you have a permit to build a building and start a program. Start with what you have now."

Mother Teresa didn't wait to pick up the dying person in the alley until she had a permit to build a facility. Heart to Heart didn't wait until we had nonprofit status to repair the YMCA in Belize. Moses didn't wait until he could hire a speech therapist. We just took the first step. The most important one.

The well-intentioned man didn't realize that he could start with whatever he had in his hand at the time. One of the things that keeps us from serving others is that we want conditions to be perfect, but they never will be. Those who need us need what we have available now. For Moses, that was enough to lead his people out of slavery. Whatever we have—a laptop, a shepherd's staff, an extra room—is enough for now.

Within a few months my tour of duty in Kosovo was over, and I returned to my family, my town, and my job. It seemed unlikely that there would be a reason for me to go back to Kosovo. But, as I began preparing this book, I could not get the Shabius out of my mind. I wanted to see how they were doing. They felt like part of my own family.

I got in touch with a missionary family who I had gotten to know during my time in Kosovo. They agreed to help me return to the Shabius. Could I bring some medicines with me for the Shabius and other families they were helping? Of course.

Would I get to see the Shabius? There was no way to let them know I was coming. When I flew into Macedonia during their civil war, and found the border crossing into Kosovo closed because of the violence, I kept asking myself "Is this worth it? What if they don't live there anymore? Why am I going to all this trouble?" I had to walk the last few miles, hiring a couple of teenagers to help me carry the boxes of medicine.

After many hours of breathing exhaust fumes I finally made it across the border and met my missionary friends, Randy and Lycia Harvey. They were a welcome sight after a very unnerving day!

The next day we headed into the mountains. When we pulled up to the Shabiu's house, Hamdi and Remzije didn't recognize me in my civilian clothes. But, when I identified myself, they treated me as a long-lost son. They rushed around their house looking for enough cups to serve tea to everyone. They offered cigarettes they had obviously rolled themselves. (Apparently my influence on them as a doctor had been limited!)

Inside the house, I looked at the wall. There was Merita's backpack. Beneath it were an Albanian and an American flag. Taped to the wall was a letter from General Sanchez telling U.S. military outposts that, if they were presented with this letter by anyone from the Shabiu family, they were to treat the Shabius with "dignity and respect."

"When you are here it feels as if my daughter has risen from the dead," Hamdi told me.

Being with them again felt like a family reunion. I brought presents for each of them—hats, sunglasses, and jewelry—and we caught up on each other's lives. They showed us the cows that had been brought to them, paid for out of the bank account we opened the year before. After a long emotional day we said our goodbyes. I wanted to see Merita's grave, so we drove there on our way out of the village. Weeds have grown up around her headstone, much like they have in and around the bombed-out buildings that surround the area. But the headstone still stands tall, a monument to the purity of a child and the grace of a community.

"She taught us to love one another," the monument says, chiseled with hard tools into the stone. I felt it chiseled into my own heart as well.

CHAPTER FOUR

GIVE WHAT YOU CAN

*Doing a thing because you feel wonderful
about it—even a work of charity—is in the
end a selfish act. We perform the work not to
feel wonderful but to know and love the other.*
Father Joe Warrillow[1]

When the devastating tsunami hit Sri Lanka and Indonesia on December 26, 2004, I knew we had to do something to help the people most affected by the disaster. Our long-term partner in responses to situations like this has been FedEx and, within hours of the news, FedEx executives called to say they had cargo planes available to take supplies to the area as soon as we were ready.

Because disasters such as hurricanes, tornadoes, earthquakes, and tsunamis occur with some regularity, relief agencies know how to react quickly and efficiently. Transportation companies like FedEx and Yellow Freight, along with pharmaceutical companies such as Johnson & Johnson, have something to offer when they partner with organizations that can get the materials into the right hands.

Responses from these companies underscore my feeling that most people want to help others. What often keeps them from doing so is that they don't know how, or that they don't think that what they have to offer would be helpful. FedEx offers us empty planes. Yellow Freight offers us empty trucks. Other organizations offer us things to put in those planes and trucks—all with the desire to serve others.

Within days we filled the FedEx planes with donated medical supplies, medicine, water, and water purification systems and headed to Sri Lanka. When we heard about areas in the region that were difficult to reach, the U.S. military let us load some of their helicopters with supplies and flew us to those remote places.

Three television crews from the Kansas City area, along with U.S. Senator Sam Brownback, accompanied us to Sri Lanka. It was an opportunity for the world to see not only the devastation but also the outpouring of help from around the world. People were suffering, and people were responding.

This outpouring was similar to the response after the terrorist attacks in New York and Washington, D.C., on September 11, 2001. On September 10, my staff and I had been in Memphis, meeting with FedEx to plan some medical airlifts for the coming year. We knew that we would be doing another airlift to China, where we had been providing medicines and conducting medical workshops for doctors and nurses throughout that country. We also knew we'd be doing an airlift to some of the former Soviet territories that were having significant problems with disease because of poverty and shortages of supplies.

We have done several relief responses in the United States— in Oklahoma where tornadoes ravaged cities, as well as in Florida after hurricanes devastated thousands of miles of homes and property. We have worked with cities throughout the country and partnered with shelters that protect women and children who have suffered from domestic violence, along with orphanages, homeless facilities, rescue missions, and food banks.

But the day after the September 11 attacks, when the country was still in a horrified daze, FedEx called and asked what they could do to help. We knew we could get supplies to the overrun hospitals quickly but we needed a staging area. FedEx offered their gigantic warehouse in Brooklyn from which we could distribute medical supplies. They also found us a facility right in Manhattan, close to the World Trade Center.

Our relationship with FedEx began with the Vietnam airlift I described earlier. I had spoken to a Rotary group in Kansas City about Heart to Heart's desire to serve the people in Vietnam, telling the Rotarians that the only thing preventing us from doing it was getting the supplies there. It was a risky project in the first place. I had been hearing about the suffering of the Vietnamese people, where hospitals didn't have enough supplies to treat the high-poverty regions, and clinics were re-using bandages, syringes, and other items that were spreading more disease.

The problem with that project was obvious. The Vietnamese still thought of as enemies to some extent. But relations between Vietnam and the United States had been improving, and it seemed the right time to do something bold. The problem was that I couldn't get anyone to agree to fly the supplies there. Politically it was too risky for the U.S. military to provide a cargo plane. I told the group this was part of what we were trying to do.

A man in the audience suggested I speak to another group he belonged to—a group of veterans. A few weeks later I told the veterans what Heart to Heart was trying to do, and one of the vets said "I know a man with airplanes." It turned out the man he was referring to was Fred Smith, the CEO of FedEx. I was not encouraged by the conversation, because I had approached FedEx before and my ideas never got past the first level.

But this vet had been in a Marine Corps unit with Fred Smith. In Vietnam. He said he'd write Smith a letter.

Within days my phone rang. It was Fred Smith. "How soon do you want to go to Vietnam?" he asked.

The first commercial plane from the United States to land in Vietnam after the war was a FedEx plane loaded with medical supplies for people we used to call our enemies.

The "big" responses to events like tsunamis and terrorist attacks started with one person doing something small. The Vietnam veteran wrote a brief letter. Everyone can do something to help relieve suffering. It may turn out to be something big, like getting FedEx planes, but that isn't the point. Very few of us have access to planes, helicopters, trucks, and warehouses. But we can all do something.

In Calcutta, I saw that even nothing was something. During the airlift and volunteer effort I described earlier, a woman felt intimidated by all of the professional people in our group.

Many of the volunteers were doctors or nurses. Others were technicians, engineers, or teachers. Still others were owners of companies who were providing supplies. Even members of the rock band Queen were with us because we were doing work with an AIDS hospice. The band was supporting an AIDS foundation named for their lead singer, Freddy Mercury, who died after a long battle with AIDS.

This particular woman did not have professional training, and she repeatedly asked herself: "What can I do? I'm just a mother. I have nothing to offer these people in need."

Her volunteer assignment in Calcutta was to work in a clinic filled with babies who were brought there to die. There were about twenty cribs in the facility, designed for one baby each. But the babies in this clinic were so emaciated and tiny that the cribs had up to four babies in each of them. Diane, our volunteer, counted at least seventy-five babies. Parents, family members, or social workers had brought the babies because there was no one else to care for them. Diane then noticed a sign on the wall.

"Do not hold the babies," the sign said.

Diane asked one of the Sisters of Charity about the sign. "If you hold one of the babies," the sister said, "the other babies sense it and cry because they want to be held too. It's just too much noise, because all of the babies can't be held."

Diane had nothing. Nothing but open space between her hands. Nothing to offer except. . . nothing.

For the rest of the day Diane picked up babies, comforted them, prayed over their tiny bodies, wept, and helped usher them from this world to the next. She had nothing to offer, which is exactly what these babies needed.

In overwhelming situations like the tsunami, it is easy to watch the news accounts and feel helpless. Even when there is access to medicine and transportation it is easy to feel that what we have to offer is too tiny to make a difference. But that sense of helplessness didn't stop one college group from doing something anyway.

An *a cappella* music group called Pointless, from Point Loma Nazarene University in San Diego, was on a singing tour up the West Coast when they saw the news about the suffering in Sri Lanka.

"We sat there and watched the images, and knew we wanted to do something," said Gerard Brown, one of the singers. "Our hearts really went out to the victims."

They all wanted to do *something*. But what? They decided that they would donate the tour proceeds, originally planned to fund the recording of their next CD. They kept doing what they were already doing. They simply rerouted some of the money they were taking in. They didn't start a tour for tsunami relief. They merely adjusted what was underway—almost nothing.

When they got back to San Diego they saw that their peers at the university were also trying to do something with almost nothing. The students arranged with the campus food service, Sodexho, to allow them to skip some of their meals, and Sodexho donated the monetary value of the meals to relief efforts. Other students conducted a "beverage fast," which meant that instead of spending money on coffee drinks or sodas, they drank water and donated the money they would have spent. The senior class decided not to go on a class trip at the end of the year and donated the money they would have spent. One of the members of the music faculty didn't have the money he wanted to donate, so he performed several benefit concerts at churches and senior citizen centers in San Diego and gave the money to the relief effort.

The chaplain at the university patched me in from Sri Lanka by phone to the university chapel, where I told them about our relief efforts. I wanted to challenge them further.

"Everyone can do something," I told them. "Even if you don't have a singing voice or a relief agency or a fleet of airplanes. Everyone has something to offer."

Many students gave money, for which I was grateful. Pointless put together a benefit concert with all of the proceeds going to tsunami relief.

Eating nothing became something. Drinking nothing became something. Going nowhere became something. Everyone can do nothing and turn it into something.

Within a few weeks, the proceeds of the benefit concert, the contribution from students, Sodexho, the beverage fast, and the cancelled senior class trip came to more than $40,000, which they gave to Heart to Heart's tsunami relief efforts. And since Heart to Heart can turn $1 into $25 worth of equivalent product, more than $1 million in aid went to tsunami victims from this small school alone.

The interesting thing about doing whatever we can, regardless of how seemingly insignificant, is that this is often precisely what the other person needs.

At a San Diego charter school in one of the city's poorest neighborhoods, some of these same principles were applied, with very interesting results. The King-Chavez charter school is in an area where the federal government took over the public elementary school because the students consistently scored below level for standardized tests required by the government. One hundred percent of the students at King-Chavez are on the government lunch program. Within a short time after the charter school began, students scored much higher on their tests than they used to—well above the required level.

"It's a school based on the principle of love," the school's director said. "We don't start with state standards and teach to them. We start with Matthew 6:13 of the Bible: 'Seek first the Kingdom of God and all these things will be added unto you.'

"We didn't come in with new programs. We started by loving [the students]. The other things came along. When the love set in, their test scores went up."

John Walton, the billionaire son of Sam Walton, founder of Wal-Mart, was a financial supporter of the King-Chavez school, as well as other innovative schools throughout the country. Walton, 58, was killed in an ultralight plane accident in 2005; a few months before his death he dropped in at the school unannounced.

"He put up the money to start this school," the director said. "But there were never any strings attached. We were always happy to see him when he came by."

After a few moments of discussion during this particular visit, Walton told the director that the school looked good and asked if there was anything else he could do for them.

"Yes," the director told him. "The bathrooms need cleaning."

Without hesitation, Walton said, "Where's the mop?" About thirty minutes later Walton reappeared, the task complete.

"We had a tensionand admiration-filled moment of staring at each other, where neither one of us said anything for about five seconds," the director said. "I was in a Holy Ghost/ poetic irony moment."

Walton left as unannounced as he had arrived.

Compared to what he *could* have done, like spread around more of his millions of dollars, some might say that he did almost nothing. It was a waste of his time and resources to mop a floor. But it was what was needed at the time. So it was everything, to Walton and the school.

Blake Nelson, a young man I have known most of his life, suffered a serious upper-leg injury as a two-year-old, and was confined to a plaster cast that started at mid-torso and went the entire length of one leg and partway down the other. He was immobilized that way for six weeks and was in considerable pain. It was impossible to keep the cast completely dry in the crotch area, so in addition to his pain and lack of mobility he had urine burns on his skin. His family lived in southern Ohio in a rented house with no air conditioning, and this was July. He was miserable, and his parents were out of ideas to keep him comfortable and occupied.

A neighbor, Mrs. Fleming, knocked at the door one afternoon. She had noticed the parents taking Blake for walks in a wagon padded with pillows, watched as the parents carried Blake up the stairs in his mummified form. Was there anything she could do to help?

Mrs. Fleming was in her eighties. She weighed about ninety pounds. Her posture was stooped from osteoporosis so that her head preceded the rest of her body. She looked frail and weak. The parents couldn't imagine how she could help with this sweaty, stir-crazy kid confined in several pounds of plaster.

Blake's mom had the wisdom to ask this question: "Did you have anything in mind?"

"Well," said Mrs. Fleming, reaching into the pocket of her house dress, "I brought something we could play with."

She pulled out a single red balloon. She blew it up, tied a knot at the end, and batted it meekly toward Blake, who was lying on a blanket on the floor of the living room. Blake lit up, laughed, and swatted it back to her. Mrs. Fleming sat in a chair across the room and hit it back to him.

Marcia, Blake's mom, left the room, sat at the kitchen table, and burst into tears. It was the first time she had heard him laugh since his accident. To her, it was the sound of hope. While Mrs. Fleming and Blake played, Marcia cleaned up dirty dishes that she had neglected because it meant leaving Blake unattended.

Playtime with Mrs. Fleming lasted about thirty minutes and it wore both of them out. As she bade Blake goodbye, he said to her: "You can come back tomorrow."

Which she did. For most of the days of his recovery.

Mrs. Fleming wasn't an orthopedic surgeon, or a bone-density specialist, or a specialist in anything. She could have easily watched that little boy go by in the wagon and said: "What a shame. I wish there was something I could do. But I have nothing to offer him."

She had space in her life. And air for a balloon. Almost nothing. Just what Blake and his parents needed. What do we live by? Small acts of service to one another.

In his novel *Jayber Crow*, the writer Wendell Berry tells of a small town whose young men were being sent off to war. Jayber, the novel's narrator, was the local barber, and people often came into his shop for something more than a haircut. They needed someone to listen to them.

Late one night, hours after he had closed the shop, Jayber sat in his own barber chair to read. A patron, Mat Feltner, wandered by and looked in the window. Mat's son Virgil was missing in action. Jayber called for Mat to come in.

Jayber and Mat chatted about meaningless things—what was happening in town, the weather, a little about the war—and then they fell into silence.

Finally, Mat said that he had had a dream about his son Virgil as a boy. In the dream it became clear to Mat that his son would not be found. In the novel, Jayber continues narrating:

"He told me this in a voice as steady and even as if it were only another day's news, and then he said, 'All I could do was hug him and cry.'

"And then I could no longer sit in that tall chair. I had to come down. I came down and went over and sat beside Mat.

"If he had cried, I would have. We both could have, but we didn't. We sat together for a long time and said not a word.

"After a while, though the grief did not go away from us, it grew quiet. What had seemed a storm wailing through the entire darkness seemed to come in at last and lie down.

"Mat got up then and went to the door. 'Well. Thanks,' he said, not looking at me even then, and went away."[2]

It doesn't have to be an airplane flying to Sri Lanka, although that helped a lot of people. Once serving others becomes part of everyday life, we can offer something as little as skipping a meal, drinking water, opening our arms, cleaning a bathroom, batting a balloon, or getting out of a chair. Virtually nothing.

To someone in particular, what seems like nothing can be everything.

CHAPTER FIVE

THINK SMALL

You can spend half of your time alone,
but you also have to be in service, or
you get a little funny.

Anne Lamott[1]

We had just pushed back from the dinner table when we heard a horn honking out front. Maybe I read something in Pete O'Neal's body language that wasn't really there. But when you're a fugitive do you ever stop being jumpy?

In my neighborhood, a honking horn is no cause for concern. It usually means someone hasn't figured out how to use the car alarm. When you're in the African bush, though, miles from any paved road, surrounded by mud and grass huts, living as Africans have lived for centuries, and you're the only one who owns a vehicle, a honking horn gets your attention.

Someone wanted to get to Pete's house badly enough to endure miles of bone-jarring cattle paths full of rain-carved ruts in the dark. Pete, his face lined with concern, looked at his wife Charlotte. She shrugged. So much was said in that wordless exchange. Who would drive out here? Why? Who knows we're here? How did they find us? What do they want?

With his graying dreadlocks pulled behind his head, his stiff back causing him to get up straight and slow, Pete looked like the aging leader in *The Lion King*. He picked up his walking stick and headed toward the sound.

The rest of us remained at the table, silent, listening to the faint hum of a Volkswagen engine accentuated by barks from countless aroused dogs. We had been talking about Pete's days as the founder of the Black Panther Party in Kansas City. We discussed his frequent run-ins with the local police and his attempt to disrupt hearings in Washington, D.C.

Pete told us about the trial where he was convicted of transporting a weapon across state lines. He told us about the death threats he received in the United States and how he escaped with the help of the American Communist Party before being sent to jail. Now, if he tried to return to the United States, he would immediately be arrested.

This was my second visit with Pete and Charlotte in Africa. At first it seemed strange to seek the help of a fugitive—a convicted felon—for a medical airlift. After all, the Black Panthers were generally feared in America when I was growing up in the 1960s and 1970s. They were trying to use violence to overthrow the U.S. government. J. Edgar Hoover, the FBI director at the time, called the Black Panthers our single most serious threat to security.

Remember the Tolstoy question in an earlier chapter: "What do men live by?" Pete and Charlotte O'Neal are perfect examples of the transformation that occurs in people's lives when they live out the answer to the Tolstoy question. The answer is by serving others.

The dining area at Pete and Charlotte's compound is extraordinarily modern, given the surroundings. It is like a patio outside a nice restaurant. There are floodlights, a satellite dish, a television/VCR, couches and easy chairs, a dart board, and a chess table. On the wall are pictures of the hosts as they live in Tanzania: Pete climbing Mount Kilimanjaro, Charlotte at an opening of a local arts center, the two of them receiving an award from the national government's arts council. There are also photos of their more distant past in the United States: Pete and Charlotte in black berets and sunglasses, holding weapons, severity etched in their faces. A boxing trophy rests on a shelf.

While Pete was checking out the horn, Charlotte maintained her conversation, but she never took her eyes off the door through which he left the room.

Soon we heard the car drive away and Pete emerged from the darkness, beaming. It had been a courier from the Kilimanjaro airport, more than an hour away. Pete held a large yellow envelope that contained a videotape labeled *American in Exile*. It was a documentary on his life, made by filmmakers at the University of California at Berkeley. This was the first copy. It had never been seen outside of the editing room in Berkeley. He gestured to all of us at the dinner table.

"Would you like to be the first to see it?"

"Maybe you and Charlotte should see it first, so you can have some privacy," I said.

"You're family," he said. "Let's watch it together." From the day I met Pete and Charlotte, I have felt like a member of their family.

I have never been to a Hollywood movie premiere. But that night, in the African bush, I saw a Tanzanian movie premiere, and I will never forget it.

It opened with scenes from Pete's neighborhood in Kansas City, where he spent his growing-up years in and out of jail. It showed the local headquarters of the Black Panther Party. It showed Panthers confronting police. It showed them feeding poor children at their schools, early in the morning. There were interviews with Pete's mother and brothers, who still live in Kansas City, and with newspaper reporters who covered the Panthers.

While we watched it together, Pete and Charlotte were in another world, transported thirty years into the past. "How did they get those pictures?" they exclaimed to one another. "How did they find that out?"

They were stunned when they saw the footage of Pete disrupting the U.S. Senate confirmation hearings of FBI director-tobe Clarence Kelly. O'Neal and Kelly were old adversaries. Kelly was Kansas City's police chief and Pete had a long history of run-ins with him.

When Kelly was about to be selected for one of the most prestigious law-enforcement positions in the country, Pete was there to shout it down, calling Kelly a menace to society. The film showed Pete, in his black beret and sunglasses, being hauled out of the confirmation room by security guards. Pete and Charlotte, seated on the couch together, shook their heads and smiled.

They believed in the struggle then and they believe in it now. But now the struggle has taken on different dimensions. Back then it included violence. No longer. Now it is service.

Pete founded the Black Panthers' Kansas City chapter in 1969. He had spent the previous several years as a petty criminal and admits now that he was probably headed for a lengthy prison term. When he heard the rhetoric of Eldridge Cleaver, Huey Newton, and other founders of the Black Panthers, something resonated with him. There was talk of an armed revolution in America—a violent overthrow of the U.S. government. There was a call for black communities to control their own destinies. There was an appetite for blacks in America to throw off their oppressors and develop a new power structure. The movement mobilized law enforcement throughout the country. Most of white America feared the Panthers, but they were fascinated by them as well.

Being a member of the Black Panther party put O'Neal in a position to help his own Kansas City community create a different approach to black life in America, he said. The local chapter put pressure on the police department by following squad cars to document any abuses. Chapter members attended public and private political meetings, demanding that the needs of their community be met. They confronted public officials, the police, businesses, and churches, sometimes violently. They made a lot of enemies with their tactics and threats. The dispute between the police and Panthers got personal, to the point where Pete even challenged Chief Clarence Kelly to a duel.

"All of the revolutionary groups of that period—the Black Panthers, the Weathermen, the Students for a Democratic Society, and others—believed that the American system of government was so corrupt that it had to be destroyed and built from the bottom up," Pete said. "We viewed the police department as an occupying army, threatening our existence, so it had to be destroyed too."

But, throughout the angry confrontations, the Panthers continued to do something else: they fed children breakfast and distributed clothing to the needy.

"Everybody likes to talk about the guns and the violence," Pete said. "But what attracted me to the Panthers is what motivates me here in Tanzania—community service. One of the great joys of my life as a Panther was to provide food for hungry kids every morning. We didn't care where we got it. For a while, the Mafia provided the food for our program. I'm sure those kids were the only ones eating sirloin steak for breakfast! The mafia liked us because we kept the police occupied and out of their hair."

In addition to feeding hungry kids, the Panthers also established a free health clinic, where a doctor, a nurse, and a pharmacist donated their time.

While the Black Panther rhetoric continued to inflame an already tense situation between blacks and the police, community service continued. Then Pete learned a lesson in Panther philosophy.

"The Panther leadership pulled me aside one day and told me to cool my personal argument with the police because it was getting in the way of lifting up the community," he said. "That was a new thought to me—that the community's needs were more important than the individual's—and I found it attractive. I became more involved in service, which had a direct effect on my materialism and my personal feuds. I started looking at the big picture."

O'Neal's run-ins with the police came to a head when he was arrested for transporting a gun across state lines. He was convicted in 1970 and sentenced to four years in prison.

"After my conviction, a police officer made it clear to me that my life in prison would be short. The officer said 'You'll come out of there in a box.' He said it with a smile on his face. I knew then that the judge had sentenced me to death."

Pete and Charlotte fled the country and lived with other members of the Panther party in exile, first in Sweden, then in Algiers. At the time they expected to return to the United States within a year. While waiting for word that he would get a new trial, the O'Neals resettled in Tanzania, then a socialist country, where they have lived since 1974.

From their very early days in Tanzania, they began putting into practice the philosophy of improving their community wherever they were. Their talk about overthrowing the United States government was replaced by a desire to improve the lives of those with whom they were living. They began farming, with no knowledge of how to farm, and connected with their neighbors. Pete started a sausage-making business. And just as they did in Kansas City, they started a community center.

"The community service bug bit us in Kansas City," Charlotte said. "Once you see how rewarding it is to live in service to others, you really can't stop."

The O'Neals conducted book drives for the local schools. Charlotte, a gifted artist, taught art classes to the women in the nearby villages.

"The art classes opened up a whole new world to these ladies," she said. "They came to our home very meek and distrusting of their abilities. Now they have confidence. Their work is on display in the cities around here. They're artists."

Seeing the devastation AIDS was having on the continent, the O'Neals showed videotapes about HIV to whoever would watch them. It wasn't culturally acceptable to talk publicly about AIDS back then, but someone needed to get the message out that the disease was preventable.

They distributed fliers the first time they showed the AIDS videotapes. More people responded than could fit in the O'Neal's home, so they hooked up a small television to a VCR and put it on top of their car, wiring it to the car's battery. Dozens of people surrounded the car to watch the video. Pete took the tapes to industrial sections of the closest city, Arusha, put his TV and VCR on top of his car, and showed the tapes to workers on their lunch breaks.

Pete and Charlotte also organized celebrations to highlight traditional dance and music of local tribal heritage. The elders of the community saw the value in these efforts and selected the O'Neals to receive a four-acre plot of land to continue developing their activities.

"That was a very significant decision," Charlotte said. "We're not Tanzanians, and we're not even part of the Wamiri tribe that dominates this area. But they saw how these things benefited the community, and they wanted us to continue."

Now the compound has several buildings to house guests, artists in residence, and exchange students. There are classes in computers, fashion design, painting, music, and dance. The Tanzanian commissioner of culture is one of the center's greatest advocates of what is now called the United African American Community Center.

One of the programs offered by the center is called Heal the Community, which gives opportunities for teenagers from Kansas City who are headed for trouble to spend time with the O'Neals and others in Tanzania.

"It is a chance for them to see their heritage and connect them to a world bigger than their neighborhoods," Pete said. "Many of these kids don't know their own history. They leave here with a lot more respect for themselves."

Many of them end their time in Tanzania with a trek up to Mount Kilimanjaro. "When they descend," he said, "they are ready to take on the world."

When I see how Pete and Charlotte live their lives for others, and think about their unlikely path from violence to service, I am reminded of the story of the Good Samaritan. Jesus tells the story in response to the question "Who is my neighbor?"

The story tells of a man walking along a road who is attacked by robbers, who beat him and leave him to die. A political leader crosses to the other side of the road to avoid the dying man. A religious leader walks by and does the same thing. But a Samaritan stops when he sees the victim. Samaritans were a hated group, viewed by the dominant culture as virtually subhuman. The Samaritan puts the dying man on his horse, takes him for medical attention, and pays the bill in advance. Jesus then asks the question "Who acted like a neighbor?"[2]

What I like about the story is that it is the most unlikely person of all who helps the beaten man. The Samaritans had rejected that day's society and revolted against it. Samaritans were considered the ultimate in corruption. They were the enemy— maybe even the Black Panthers of their day. The story is so powerful because it is an "enemy" responding to a person in need. It teaches that our "neighbor" is whoever is in need and, further, that service to others can happen in most unlikely situations.

Thomas Keating says that service, which comes from a heart of love, "knows no political or religious boundaries. . . . In the person of the Good Samaritan, the [boundaries] are swept away." According to Keating, the parable means that "Everyone must be concerned about everyone else."[3]

I first heard about Pete when I was trying to drum up support for a medical airlift to Arusha, a sister city to my home town of Kansas City. Tanzania is one of the poorest countries on the poorest continent in the world. Heart to Heart wanted to take much-needed medical supplies to hospitals and clinics there. After a meeting in downtown Kansas City with some business and political leaders, the mayor pulled me aside.

"When you go to Arusha, I want you to contact a distant cousin of mine," said Mayor Emmanuel Cleaver. I knew he was a relative of Eldridge Cleaver's, one of the founders of the Black Panther party in Oakland, California. But the mayor told me about another cousin named Pete O'Neal.

I contacted Pete, and he invited me to stay in his guest house while I was looking for appropriate sites for our airlift. I didn't know what to expect when I arrived. Mayor Cleaver had told me some things about Pete, and I did a little reading about him. I was a teenager during the race riots of the 1960s and I remembered how I had feared the Black Panthers. Every white person I knew was terrified of them. The closer I got to my first encounter with Pete the more apprehensive I became.

When I got to his house, my first thought was, "So this is the life of a celebrity fugitive."

One building has a mural with the faces of those who gained freedom and rights for blacks in America. Malcolm X, whose book *The Autobiography of Malcolm X* energized and fueled Pete's beliefs, appears front and center. Martin Luther King, Jr., Nat Turner, John Brown, Sojourner Truth, and Harriet Tubman are also there. The building where Pete and Charlotte sleep has a painting of a ferocious-looking black panther.

I have to confess that I was skeptical about associating Heart to Heart with a felon on the run who had been so radically and militantly committed to the overthrow of the U.S. government. Were the O'Neals going to use this project for some personal political gain? I didn't know if I could trust them.

When I talked with Pete, however, I felt instant rapport. Pete's personal warmth is matched only by the intensity of his views. That first night we talked well into the next morning about the beliefs each of us hold dear. We are both idealists and activists. Both of us are well aware of the problems and injustices in the world around us. Pete had chosen to address these problems through violence.

He had advocated the revolutionary overthrow of a political system he felt was unjust. I had chosen to work within the system, and addressed the role of the individual in changing the world.

As different as we were, and as different as were the paths we had chosen, one thing was the same. We thought the world needed improving. We talked about politics, race relations, global affairs, and how both as young men dreamed big dreams, thinking we could change the world.

I told him about Heart to Heart, about the impromptu speech I gave at a Rotary Club meeting, and how we now go to disaster areas around the world to provide medical supplies. I told him that it gives both corporate leaders and private individuals an opportunity to find meaning. I told him about providing immediate aid to victims of tornadoes, floods, hurricanes, and riots in the United States as well as to those suffering from natural or economic disasters throughout the world.

I told him about my philosophy that serving others is how we find meaning and significance in our lives, and about the three points I repeat to everyone:

- Everyone has something to give.
- Everyone can start where they are.
- Most people are willing to serve others when they see the need and opportunity.

Pete told me about his and Charlotte's efforts in Tanzania. He told me that they had abandoned violence as a means for change and decided to make an impact where they lived. There were similarities in the struggles we face to accomplish our goals. Many have to do with what happens when it appears we are at an impasse, where our resources simply can't stretch far enough to meet the desperate needs of those around us.

"There is a law of the universe that comes into play at that point," Pete said. "I learned it from Charlotte, who may have gotten it from her religious upbringing in Kansas City. It is simply: "Give, and you will be cared for. Don't give, and it will all be taken away." I understood the sentiment.

Pete cited several examples of how this law worked in their community center. They started their computer class with about a dozen people crowded around one computer. Within a few weeks local businesses and governments were providing them with more computers. Now they have an entire classroom with a computer on every desk. To fully appreciate this, you have to realize how far they are from city life. The region around them still has an uneven electrical supply. Water for the local villages is still collected and carried from a village well. The only employment is in hard labor, raising corn, bananas, coffee, or flowers.

The popularity and success of the computer training classes has been duplicated with instruction in music, languages, dance, and art. As word gets out about the efforts at the Community Center, people from the area look for ways they can contribute. "Seeing it all come back gives you the strength to keep going for another day," Pete said.

I knew exactly what he meant. People at Heart to Heart had similar feelings when responding to an overwhelming hurricane in New Orleans, a devastating tornado in Oklahoma, and a record-setting earthquake in Pakistan. We start as if we have what we need, even though we don't, and there is always enough to proceed. It almost never happens, though, if we wait until we have enough supplies or resources or volunteers to respond to a need. *If we wait, there's never enough to act. If we act, there's always enough.* As Pete said, it seems to be a law of the universe.

Rabbi Harold Kushner writes from a similar perspective in his book *How Good Do We Have to Be?* Helping others, Kushner says, "is not like a bank account that is depleted as it is given away, where every dollar of love can only be spent once. Love is not like a buffet line where the person in front of you threatens to take too much and leave too little for you. . . . Whenever we 'give away' our love, God replenishes it so that we become the channel of His love flowing to all of His children, a channel that never runs dry."[4]

That first night Pete and I initiated a friendship and a partnership. He helped us identify places in Tanzania that need medical supplies most. He also helped me see the value of a person living out his passion to serve others right where he was, despite the fact that he is unable to return home.

"Where would I be able to do what I do if I were in the United States?" he asked. "I often wonder how my life would be different if we hadn't gotten in that car, sneaked out of Kansas City, and escaped through New York. Actually, I think I know the answer. I'd be dead."

Rabbi Kushner says that, at a rational level, giving ourselves to others doesn't change our past, "but at the irrational level, where our souls live, it does introduce us to our better, nobler self."[5] Pete was clearly living out his better self in Tanzania.

At the end of my initial visit, Pete said he had a question for me.

"Gary, we have talked all night about what motivates us, gets us inspired, keeps us going," he said. "For me it started as a political movement. But that movement is over. Most of the beliefs that got me started in this have proven to be ineffective. So I have a question for you: What 'ism' we should give our lives to?"

There was great intensity in his voice.

Pete told me of the transformation in his life when he gave himself over to an "ism." In his case it was socialism. In the early days of his transformation, the socialist life seemed ideal. People did what they could for the good of the larger society, and everyone's needs were met, according to the philosophy.

He pointed back to that incident where the leaders of the party told him he needed to set aside his personal issues with the Kansas City police in order to serve the larger black community in Kansas City.

"It was a philosophy completely opposite to the way I was living," Pete said. "I was the most materialistic, self-indulgent person on the earth, and I didn't care how I got my clothes or jewelry or cars." Marxist thought opened his eyes to a world bigger than himself. It motivated and energized him. Then he saw its collapse through greed and hypocrisy.

"It was the 'ism' that pulled me from the brink," he said, "and then I saw that it didn't work. So what do you replace it with when that's gone?"

We talked at length about the philosophies and flaws of communism, socialism, capitalism, anarchism, and all of the other social systems the human race has tried. Neither one of us could identify a system worth giving our lives to.

Here I was, with a guy who believed he could change the world by overthrowing the dominant political force. When he realized he wasn't going to change the world or even the United States, he focused his energy on changing the community in which he settled in faraway Tanzania. Tied to his big question —What "ism" should we give our lives to? — was why I did what I did with Heart to Heart. What were my motives, what made me want to change the world, and what was my "ism?"

It's a fair question, one we all need to ask ourselves from time to time. Why do we do what we do? What makes us think we are making a difference? What makes us think we *can* make a difference? What do we live by?

The philosopher Huston Smith addressed the "isms" issue that Pete and I were discussing. He said that communism and progressivism, the most dominant "isms" of the twentieth century, left out a crucial component.

"Neither filled the spiritual hollow in the human makeup," he said. "Progress has turned into something of a nightmare. The campaign against ignorance has expanded our knowledge of nature, but science cannot tell us what we should give our lives to."

As for communism, "Marx saddled his movement with a bloody-mindedness the likes of which history has rarely seen. . . . The Marxist record on compassion is no better than its record on truth."[6]

I told Pete I have concluded that every ideology will ultimately fail. Some may seem to hold more promise for justice and fairness than others, but in the end they will all fail.

"Everyone needs a sense of purpose in their lives that transcends their daily routines," I said. "I believe our purpose is to give of ourselves according to our ability to give, and according to our neighbor's need. That's the only way we can find meaning in our lives on this earth. It's not about making money or acquiring power. It's about serving others. That's what we're here to do. That's my 'ism.'"

It's not bumper-sticker material, but it adequately describes looking past my own personal circumstances to see how we all fit into the bigger picture.

Pete thought about that for a long time, and then nodded. It seemed as if we agreed at a deep level. Unlike him, I didn't get my start in an effort to overthrow the power structure of the country, but I did experience a different kind of overthrow.

The culture that surrounded me as a young person was dominated by self-interest and self-indulgence. While our wealthy culture got wealthier, I saw people suffering, both in the United States and elsewhere. I simply was not satisfied with making more money, achieving more goals, and accumulating more things. I saw that there was a better, more fulfilling way to live, and that living for yourself is its own type of slavery. Living to serve others is a kind of liberation that I would call revolutionary.

I believe it is possible, and even desirable, to live to serve others.

That night at Pete's compound we talked the language of the heart. We probed and prodded each other's assumptions and beliefs. He was as committed to doing the right thing as any person I've ever met.

I knew I had made a true friend when we said goodbye at the airport a few days later. As we got out of the van and started to walk into the terminal, he asked me to stay behind for a moment. There was something he wanted me to do. Here it comes, I thought The Big Ask. He needs money or something.

After a lengthy silence, Pete put his hands on my shoulders. "Could you do me a favor?"

I am used to people asking me for favors. Sometimes they want free medical advice. Sometimes they want samples of medicines. Sometimes they want sophisticated equipment, like CT scanners for their local hospitals or clinics, which are a little tougher to procure. I assumed Pete wanted me to get some vaccinations for the local school children or supplies for the local clinic. Maybe he wanted me to build a hospital on the compound.

"I will do whatever I can," I assured Pete.

"My father is dying of cancer in Kansas City, and I can't visit him because of my legal status," Pete said. "I want you to visit him for me and tell him how I'm doing. You don't have to take him anything or give him anything. Just go to him and do what you've done with me. Just be you. Talk to him. Laugh with him. There's a family joke I want you to talk about. For years I have joked about being a Golden Gloves boxing champion. Can you make something up and keep the story going?"

That was it? Visit his sick dad? Talk about boxing? That's all he wanted me to do? Tears filled my eyes. Pete would never see his dad again. But I could go to his father and share something of his son, who I had come to know and love.

"Of course I'll do it," I said. "I'd be honored." I stuck out my hand to shake his.

"No," Pete insisted. "We're friends. We're brothers." And with that he gave me a big hug.

I left Tanzania thinking about the juxtaposition of Pete's two questions.

Here was a man who had committed his life to revolutionizing the world, and he ended up in deepest Africa. We had talked all night about the "isms" of humanity's best intelligence. Macro systems. Big Picture ideas.

But we don't live each day in macro systems. We live in micro systems. Frame by frame. Moment by moment.

How can we bridge the two? How do we find meaning in our lives, commit to something bigger than ourselves, in a frameby-frame life? By doing small things, like visiting the dying father of a fugitive revolutionary. By doing something for someone that he can't do for himself. We can start where we are.

Sometimes we get paralyzed by the world's problems and needs and how inadequate we are to solve them. But we can all do *something*, no matter how small. Heart To Heart started with a small project. Pete's transformation started with something just as small.

I couldn't solve the unemployment problem in Tanzania, or the AIDS epidemic, or any of the other major challenges the people there are facing. I couldn't help Pete change his world. But I *could* visit his father. True service begins by thinking small.

I called Pete's dad when I got back to the United States. I told him his son was doing great things for others. I told him he was the heavyweight boxing champion of Tanzania. I told him that his son loved him very much. He seemed happy to hear about Pete. I asked if I could come by to visit, but he wasn't doing well enough to have visitors. He died a short time later.

Sometimes people don't consider serving another person because the problems of the world seem too big. What's one act of service going to change?

Everything.

CHAPTER SIX

BE THERE

*We don't have to find the cure for cancer
to make a difference to the world. . . we only
have to share our lives with other people.*
Rabbi Harold Kushner[1]

I have always been an advocate of crossing lines that keep people from helping one another. Those lines may be intangible barriers such as social status, or physical ones, such as an ocean. I am convinced that one of the reasons certain groups of people aren't cared for is that we simply never think of them. That's why, on many of our airlifts, we try to find groups of people to visit that would not be obvious. Then, when our volunteers return to their home towns, they are much more aware of those who are out on the margins of our attention. Once people see how easy it is to cross cultural and economic lines on these airlifts, many readily do the same as part of their lifestyles when they get home.

There were obvious lines to cross in the facilities run by Mother Teresa in Calcutta. The people there were suffering, and they were placed in specific facilities everyone could easily find.

But there is also a village outside of Calcutta inhabited by people with leprosy, that horrifying disease that destroys flesh. When we found out about this leper colony, and that people there were abandoned and feared, we took all of our volunteers to the village, hired a group of musicians and entertainers, and threw the residents a party.

We did the same thing in Vietnam, where leprosy is still a serious health issue. We brought the Vietnamese village the best grain we could find for their cooking and provided school supplies for each child. The religious people in our group prayed blessings over those who requested prayers.

I got this idea after hearing the great preacher and sociologist Tony Campolo talk about being in a greasy spoon in Honolulu at three in the morning, unable to sleep because of the time change in traveling from the East Coast. While he was sitting at the counter eating a donut and drinking bad coffee, three boisterous prostitutes came in.

"Tomorrow's my birthday," one announced. "I'm going to be thirty-nine."

One of the women scoffed at her and mockingly asked if she wanted someone to throw her a party.

"Why do you have to be so mean? I was just telling you, that's all. I don't want anything from you. Why should you give me a birthday party? I've never had a birthday party in my whole life. Why should I have one now?"

That conversation gave Campolo an idea. When the women left, he asked the man behind the counter "Do they come in here every night?"

"Yeah," the man said.

"The one who sat next to me, does she come here every night?"

"Yeah, that's Agnes. She's here every night. Why do you want to know?"

"Because I heard her say that tomorrow was her birthday," I said. "What do you think about us throwing a birthday party for her, right here, tomorrow night?"

The employee liked the idea and called to his wife in the kitchen.

"Get out here. This guy's got a great idea. Tomorrow is Agnes's birthday. This guy wants us to go in with him and throw a birthday party for her, right here, tomorrow night!"

His wife loved the idea.

"That's wonderful," she said. "Agnes is one of those people who is really nice and kind, and nobody ever does anything nice and kind for her."

"I'll come back here tomorrow morning about two-thirty and decorate the place," Campolo said. "I'll even buy the birthday cake."

"No way," said the man behind the counter. "The birthday cake's my thing. I'll make the cake."

At two-thirty the next morning, Campolo was back at the diner. He had picked up some paper decorations at a store and made a big sign that said "Happy Birthday, Agnes!" He decorated the diner from one end to the other.

The diner's owners must have gotten the word out on the streets of Honolulu, because by 3:15 nearly every prostitute in Honolulu was in that diner. Wall to wall prostitutes, and Campolo!

At 3:30 the door swung open and in came Agnes and her friend, and everyone in the diner screamed "Happy Birthday!"

Campolo said he had never seen anyone so flabbergasted, so stunned and shaken. Her mouth fell open and her legs seemed to buckle, he said. Her friend grabbed her arm to steady her. As she was led to one of the stools at the counter they all sang "Happy Birthday" to her. When they got to the part where they sang "Happy Birthday dear Agnes," Campolo said it looked as if she were going to cry. But when they brought out the cake with the candles on it, she broke down and wept.

Everyone badgered her into blowing out the candles, after which she kept staring at the cake. Finally someone handed her a knife to cut it. She continued to stare while it got quiet in the diner.

She asked if it was all right to not eat it right away. The owner shrugged his shoulders.

"Sure it's OK!" he said. "If you want to keep the cake, keep the cake. Take it home if you want to."

"I just live a couple of doors down," Agnes said. "I want to take the cake home and show it to my mother, OK? I'll be right back. Honest!"

She got off the stool, Campolo said, picked up the cake, and carrying it like it was the Holy Grail, walked slowly toward the door. When the door closed, he said there was a stunned silence in the place.[2]

When I heard Campolo tell that story, I committed my own heart to seek out diners where I could and provide cakes to people who generally don't get birthday parties.

That's why we go to the leprosy clinics. No one else will touch these people. And they are dying from being unable to feel touch any longer! That sounds like a lot of people without leprosy, doesn't it? Everyone encounters someone every day, often across cultural lines, who could benefit from a gesture that says "I see you. You matter."

It is not always possible, or even necessary, to cross major cultural or physical barriers to serve others. Sometimes the people are right next to us and need something very small. Sometimes all they need is for us to be present with them—simply be there.

Anne Lamott, in her book *Traveling Mercies*, said "When all is said and done, all you can do is to show up for someone in crisis, which seems so inadequate. But then when you do, it can radically change everything. Your there-ness, your stepping into a line of vision, can be life giving, because often everyone else is in hiding. So you come to keep them company when it feels like the whole world is falling apart, and your being there says that just for this moment, this one tiny piece of the world is OK, or is at least better."[3]

That's how it seemed when we visited the leprosy clinics. The people there hide, or are hidden, from the world. But it's easy to see them if we're looking. We don't have to cure their leprosy. Our presence, our "there-ness," will alleviate a different affliction. By keeping them company for a little while we show they aren't invisible. Being ignored, or unseen, is a terrible disease. Feeling unworthy is another one.

In his book *Father Joe*, Tony Hendra tells of being a conflicted young man who was behaving badly as he battled internal demons. Off and on he visited a monk in a monastery, first as a punishment and then by choice. One desperate night Hendra was contemplating suicide because he thought he had committed an unforgivable sin. In the middle of the night he pounded on the monastery door in search of the monk, Father Joe. The monk at the gate reluctantly went to find Father Joe, who had obviously been sleeping.

"He did nothing but listen," Hendra wrote. "He made no attempt to calm me or cool the heat of this new development in the insane life of this insane child. He didn't try to explain why I was feeling these things, why what seemed so catastrophic was actually normal, common for my age. . . . He didn't try to shock me out of my funk or manhandle me for my own good with tough love. He called down no higher powers to intercede on my behalf, nor did he invite me to join him in prayer."

Father Joe did not try to give Hendra answers, or even tell Hendra that everything was going to be all right.

"He took my condition head on, as seriously as I took it," Hendra said. "Tonight there was just a desperate boy on a cold and lonely cinder spinning through a meaningless universe who'd come running across the Home Counties in a waking nightmare."

Father Joe found a place at the monastery for Hendra to stay, and sat at the edge of the bed until Hendra fell asleep.

"How long he sat there I have no idea. Two minutes? Two hours?" Hendra said. "Peace descended like snowflakes. My terror receded until it was far out to sea. The dark hordes were nowhere to be seen. Sweet oblivion came and I slept."[4]

Father Joe didn't provide answers. That isn't what Hendra needed. Father Joe provided *presence*. He knew that the best response in this situation was to be there.

After Father Joe died, Hendra read his obituary and was surprised by the statement that Father Joe had "touched the lives of so many people, in England and abroad, in his own Church and not . . . it is hard to give full weight to the extent of his pastoral influence."

In his self-centered arrogance, Hendra had assumed that he was the only person Father Joe had influenced so deeply.

"Father Joe had undertaken not just a few, or even a few dozen, but hundreds of such life-altering voyages," Hendra wrote. "It was immensely disarming and engaging to be treated as if you were the only one in his life; but then, for the time you were with him, you were. He loved the one he was with: spiritually promiscuous, utterly discreet."

After Hendra expressed surprise that Father Joe had these kinds of "listening" relationships with many others, one of the monks at the monastery said "Ah yes—everyone thought they were Joe's best friend."

"And all of us were right," Hendra said. "We all were."[5] Father Joe's example was the kind of experience I had when

I returned to Kosovo as a civilian, a year or so after I had served there as an Army Reserve doctor. I was driving with some friends at night and one of them asked if I would mind going with them to look in on a woman who had been very ill. My friends had been helping her and her family off and on, and they wanted to check on her health while I was there.

A series of very bumpy roads led to this family's threeroom cinderblock house at the edge of a community. There were children everywhere. The clothes on some of them were filthy and ragged. The father came out and shook our hands. I could tell immediately that something was not right with him. The story, my friends told me, is that he was in a room gassed by Serbian military and he had suffered brain damage. The fellow was cheerful enough but seemed childlike.

Inside the house I heard moaning and yelling. I followed the noise and was startled by what I saw. Two young adults lay on the floor under blankets. One, who was deformed and appeared unable to sit up, stared at his visitors with the gaze of a frightened horse,

frozen in place, his blanket soiled. The other, apparently agitated by
the newcomers, moaned and shouted at the ceiling while repeatedly
slamming himself into the wall.

The person in the most discomfort physically was the mother
of these two incapacitated people. She was the wife of the brain-
damaged man, and the mother of some of the children who were
crawling in and out of my friends' van outside.

She sat in a chair much too large for her shrinking frame and
I could tell right away that she was dying. Through an Albanian
interpreter I asked her if she was in pain. Yes, she said. Her sister,
standing nearby, told me that she had breast cancer. I took her vital
signs and listened to her lungs. They were filled with fluid and she
was getting very little air. Her pulse and blood pressure were very
weak. She had more than breast cancer.

I talked with her about her children. The two in the other room
were born with significant physical and mental defects, she told me.
The children playing outside were fine physically, but they had so
much energy that they were driving her crazy.

After giving her some pain medication I asked her if she knew
how sick she was. She did. She was well aware of her condition, and
very afraid.

"Afraid of what?" I asked.

"Afraid of what will happen to my children when I am gone,"
she said. Her sister assured her that they would be cared for.

Once her pain eased a bit, I asked if there was anything I could
do for her. Because we were communicating through an interpreter,
I wasn't exactly sure I understood her answer. She pointed toward
the open door and said "I want to go out there." Or perhaps she was
pointing to the sky and saying "I want to go away."

Just in case, my friend and I carried her, in her chair, out into
the night. She gazed up at the sky, black and scattered with stars. I
knew that, as a doctor, I could not do another thing for her. But as
a human being, a fellow resident from another side of the planet, I

could remain by her side a while longer. We talked a little more about her journey ahead of her.

"I want to go to heaven," she said.

"I'll see you there," I told her. The kids playing outside settled down a little, and the dogs stopped barking. The only sound was of the one son still hitting the wall indoors, and an occasional bellow from the family cow tied up nearby. The woman and I sat side by side, gazing at the stars. Her pain subsided a little, and I told her goodbye. She died a few hours later.

Sometimes the greatest thing we can share with another human being is our "space." True hospitality, Henri Nouwen writes, isn't just about having someone come into our homes.

"It is possible," Nouwen writes, "for men and women . . . to offer an open and hospitable space where strangers can cast off their strangeness and become our fellow human beings."[6]

Hospitality is not just opening up physical space. It opens up personal space as well. In addition to "making room" or "cleaning up" around a home or an apartment for someone, true hospitality makes room in our lives as well.

Lauren Winner, in her book *Mudhouse Sabbath,* speaks of her resistance to having people over to her apartment unless it was spotless and orderly. Given her housekeeping skills and how cramped her apartment was, that meant people were never invited in. Then she realized that she was not thinking about hospitality as "sharing space," but as "showing off." She wanted everyone to see how perfect her place was.

"If I'm inviting someone over for tea," she wrote, "it might be nice if I emptied the kitchen trash can and didn't leave dirty clothes all over the bathroom floor. But to be a hostess, I'm going to have to surrender my notions of *Good Housekeeping* domestic perfection. I will have to set down my pride and invite people over even if I have not dusted. This is tough."

She then broadened that concept to include her life, not just her apartment. Before she "invited someone in" her life, she wanted to make sure her life was orderly and perfect. Which, of course, was never.

"Just as I'd rather welcome guests into a cozy apartment worthy of *Southern Living*, I'd rather show them a Lauren who is perfect and put-together and serene," she said.

Having guests and visitors come into an apartment or a life, "if we do it right, is not an imposition, because we are not meant to rearrange our lives for our guests—we are meant to invite our guests to enter into our lives as they are," she said.

Like most of our homes or apartments, our interior lives are not going to ever be "ready," or perfect, for someone else to come in and share. But that's where we live.

"I ought to be able to risk issuing the occasional invitation," she writes.[7]

I'm not talking about throwing parties, necessarily. I'm just talking about the value of being with someone who is tired of being alone. This is part of serving others. As Lauren Winner writes, it takes a different kind of thinking, but once that internal shift is made, it becomes easier than we thought. Creating space for others does not mean we have to have everything perfect first. We just have to be open to seeing others, and what we have to offer them, in a different light.

Hospitality is a way of looking at our fellow human beings, and it can be expressed in countless ways. The best way to express it, in my opinion, is simply to be with the person in need. They might not need anything other than the space you can create in your life for them.

The people in the leprosy village outside of Calcutta didn't really "need" a concert. But they did need someone to say "I notice you." The children in the leprosy village in Vietnam probably didn't "need" the school supplies we gave them. They needed to be acknowledged.

The woman in Kosovo was made a little more comfortable by the medicine I gave her, but what she needed was some assurance that her children would be cared for, along with someone to sit with her on her last evening on earth and talk with her about heaven. That's creating space.

"Hospitality means primarily the creation of a free space where the stranger can enter and become a friend instead of an enemy," Nouwen wrote.[8]

In the movie *Hotel Rwanda* the main character, Paul Rusesabagina, played by Don Cheadle, is a hotel manager at a time when a rebellion boils over and members of the rebel Hutu tribe begin to slaughter those in the Tutsi tribe. It is gruesome and intense and infuriating to see the lives go to waste through political corruption and cowardice, but the redeeming moments of the movie are when the manager, whose hotel is already full to the brim with refugees seeking safety, continues to make more room for those who have no place else to go.

More than a million Rwandan people were massacred in three months. Rusesabagina was able to save his own family and about a thousand others. He was not a politician, a soldier or a

U.N. peacekeeper. In fact, he was a member of the Hutu tribe, and the people seeking refuge in his hotel were Tutsis, or "cockroaches," as they were called by the militia. He was merely a man who could create space. He was the incarnation of hospitality. What he did was *be there* for the people who were afraid.

The way the movie ends illustrates his philosophy. He and his wife have just found their nieces in a refugee camp and head for the bus that will take them to safety. They have been told that there is room only for his immediate family.

"Do you think there will be room for all of us?" an aid worker asks.

"There's always room," he says.[9]

He knew what he was talking about. He had been making room all along. The tagline under the movie's title was, "When the world closed its eyes, he opened his arms." That would be something all of us could be known for, don't you think?

Mother Teresa was a foreign-born nun in her late thirties, heading up a girls' boarding school in Calcutta. But on her way through the city, she could not help being overwhelmed by the sight of people abandoned in the streets to die.

"Under the impact of those grim sights she felt a call to a new form of vocation," wrote the psychologist James Fowler. "A ministry of presence, service, and care to the abandoned, the forgotten, the hopeless."

In a world that gives attention and resources to those who can "contribute" to society, Fowler asks "What could be less relevant than carrying these dying persons into places of care, washing them, caring for their needs, feeding them when they are able to take nourishment, and affirming by word and deed that they are loved and valued people of God?

"But in a world that says people only have worth if they pull their own weight and contribute something of value, what could be *more* relevant?"[10]

Mother Teresa didn't create a movement, or a corporation, or a political action group. She saw someone and created space.

One of the most dramatic examples of someone "being there" came about during Christmas 1995 in the city of Lawrence, Massachusetts. Just two weeks before, the local textile manufacturing plant, Malden Mills, burned to the ground. The plant's 3,000 employees faced the prospect of having no jobs during the holidays. In addition, everyone assumed that the owner would take this opportunity to move the entire operation out of town, probably to a developing country with inexpensive labor. The city feared losing its greatest economic asset.

But, a day after the fire, the owner, Aaron Feuerstein, grandson of the company's founder, announced that all employees would continue to receive their salaries despite having no place to work, and that he would rebuild the plant on that very site.

News accounts quoted him saying, "It would be unconscionable to put three thousand people on the streets and deliver a death blow to the city of Lawrence. Maybe on paper my company is worth less to Wall Street, but I can tell you that it is worth more."

Rabbi Harold Kushner, in his book *Living a Life That Matters*, said acts like this occur when we see events and people from a point of view other than our own.

"The voice that commanded Aaron Feuerstein to rebuild Malden Mills, the voice that commands us to volunteer our time at a homeless shelter, the voice that urges us to put the needs and feelings of our family ahead of our own, is the voice of God," he said.

When we do things for others, we are learning "to see the world from God's point of view."[11]

Feuerstein decided he would "be there" for his employees and his community. It might have been easier to move the operation. It certainly would have been cheaper. He remained in town.

Sometimes we feel helpless when it comes to serving others because it seems that we can't *do* anything. We have all heard others say "Don't just stand there, *do* something." That's not always what people need. Often, they simply need someone to create space for them.

In other words, "Don't just do something, *stand* there!"

CHAPTER SEVEN

LOSE TO WIN

*We knew that we had nothing to lose
except for our so ridiculously naked lives.*
                                Viktor Frankl[1]

Tom and Dana Larson were used to winning. Tom was an advertising copywriter in the Denver area, producing successful ad campaigns for McDonald's, Safeway, and the Denver International Airport. He got the attention of the advertising world with his "Normal People Like Us, Too," campaign for the Denver Art Museum. For his successes, he won the Denver Advertising Federation's Best in Show award.

Dana Larson, Tom's wife, led recruitment teams for accounting and high-tech companies in the Denver area. She had established herself as a skillful, and driven, head hunter. Dana got the employees she wanted and the deals she wanted.

The problem was, the Larsons were unhappy. Even the thrill of Tom's winning the advertising award was short-lived.

"I went into the office that next Monday," Tom said, "and there we all were, sitting around the table discussing accounts, just as we had every other Monday. Nothing had changed, and I realized it was never going to change."

So he quit.

He wrote freelance advertising copy to pay the bills. He wrote a novel. Dana continued as a head hunter. But they still felt something was missing in their lives.

In church one weekend, the Larsons thought they had found the answer. Their minister told of his desire to send someone for a year to work with a small church in the Dominican Republic. That was the answer to their malaise, Tom and Dana thought. They volunteered and were accepted.

Dana quit her job.

They moved to the Dominican Republic. Their Spanish skills weren't great, the living conditions were harsh, they were sick much of the time, and the church they served was both legalistic and judgmental. They were miserable.

"As pathetic as this sounds, sometimes Dana and I would drive to the Santo Domingo airport, sit in the air-conditioned Wendy's restaurant, and longingly watch people board planes headed for the United States," Tom said, shaking his head in embarrassment. "We couldn't wait to get out of there."

They returned to the United States a year later, wondering why they had gone to the Dominican Republic in the first place. Two months after their return, Hurricane Georges swept through the Caribbean and devastated the area where the Larsons had lived.

"I watched the news coverage and called the Dominican people I knew," Tom said, emotion rising in his voice. "I had this overwhelming sense of needing to help them. I don't know why, but I felt they were my family."

His Denver church helped finance immediate needs, including shelter for some of the residents. But Tom believed he could do more because he had been there. He just didn't know what.

A local scientist approached Tom after church one day and said he had been experimenting to find an inexpensive way to purify water. The scientist wanted to know if Tom thought the people in the Dominican Republic could use it. The system included chlorine, carbon filtering, reverse osmosis, and UV light, and it could work with the existing water supply of the community.

"I had seen the need for clean water there even before the hurricane, but hadn't really thought about it," Tom said. "Come on, what could I do? I was an English major!"

Now Tom and his scientist friend took the system to the Dominican Republic and installed it in the church where the Larsons had worked the previous year. They tested it repeatedly and it had zero contaminants. When word got out there was clean water available at the church, people flocked to it. Soon the church was distributing a thousand gallons a day.

This church had formerly had such a bad reputation that drivers would stop to honk their horns and yell abusive language at the parishioners during services. The yelling stopped when clean water arrived.

"The response from the community was overwhelming," Tom said. "They used to call the church names for being judgmental and elitist. This changed all that. In addition, it made the church itself look outward."

Tom got to thinking. Years of neglect had made the municipal water systems unsafe in the Dominican Republic. In the cities and larger communities there is an underground infrastructure to supply water, but the pipes carrying that water are defective and porous. That, combined with an inadequate sewage and sanitation system, exposes the water to contamination that seeps through the ground. Well water in the outlying barrios is even worse. Hurricane Georges had further damaged the underground systems.

International health organizations say that contaminated drinking water is the chief source of many communicable diseases that are the leading cause of death in affected areas. Most people there have some kind of intestinal parasite. Even when the parasites don't cause death, they cause other long-term health problems. One doctor said, "If we treated everyone tomorrow for their intestinal parasites, by the next day they would be sick again."

Tom talked to the people of the Dominican church about helping install other purification systems if they could get the financial support. Then Tom returned to his Denver church and shared his idea with the elders. Soon he started a nonprofit organization called Healing Waters International.

Tom and Dana sold their home in posh Evergreen, Colorado, and moved to smaller quarters in Golden, living off equity while they tried to develop the organization and raise some money. They got financial backing quickly, mostly from individuals. They hired Dominicans, as well as a couple of Americans who were also struggling to find their place in the world. Tom worked on developing a lower-maintenance system and on raising money. Dana concentrated on logistics, finance, and incorporating the group as a nonprofit organization.

Within months, Healing Waters was installing systems in Dominican Republic churches at a rate of one per month.

"It had the effect of building bridges between churches and their communities," Tom said. "I thought of it as an agent of healing, both physically and socially."

Most of the sites now have a constant flow of people at the church distribution centers. People come with five-gallon jugs or whatever they can find. The churches charge a fraction of the amount charged in local stores. One church dispensed more than 60,000 gallons of clean water in one of its first months of operation.

A resident of a community where there is a Healing Waters site said that virtually everyone in her village gets their water from the church.

"We never had safe water before," she said. "Our children were sick all the time. They drink this water and they are no longer sick."

For Tom, the Healing Waters effort is the outgrowth of his frustration with his career and with the year he and Dana spent in the Dominican Republic as church volunteers.

"We are in the middle of something that is so much bigger than we are," he said. He listed the former careers of his staff to make his point. "Just look at us. An advertising guy, a software consultant, a tailor, a waiter, and a used car salesman. What are we doing? What business do we have trying to pull this off?"

Healing Waters has expanded into Mexico, Guatemala, and other parts of Latin America. They plan to install purification systems in Africa as soon as possible.

"My dream is that a poor person will be able to go into any village church *on any continent* for clean, affordable water," Tom said.

Remember, Healing Waters started from the desire to have a more meaningful life, and that desire led to an apparent failure. When Tom and Dana thought they had found the answer, things didn't work out. During their first stay in the Dominican Republic, they were spiritually in the place Robert Pirsig describes in his book *Zen and the Art of Motorcycle Maintenance*: "This is the zero moment of consciousness," he writes. "Stuck. No answer. Honked. Kaput. It's a miserable experience emotionally. You're losing time. You're incompetent. You don't know what you're doing. You should be ashamed of yourself."[2]

They felt they had tried and lost. Which is the point. Serving others doesn't always turn into a big success story.

Healing Waters may not grow any bigger than it is right now. It might not survive the next few years. But the Larsons tried something even though the odds were against them. Their efforts seemed pointless at times. But they weren't after a result, they were responding to an inner need to serve others. When things looked bleak, they served anyway.

A few years ago I ran for U.S. Congress. The climate seemed right for a moderate voice, and I believed I had something to contribute to the dialogue in Washington, based on having started my own businesses and run a successful nongovernmental agency. I looked at politics as a different kind of service and a way to serve more people. My advisors were for it, and a campaign staff came together quickly.

Probably I was naïve, thinking I could run a campaign on the issues and on my experience. I didn't know that to win a race like this I would have to demonize my opponents and have them demonize me. I didn't even make it to the primary.

It was disappointing to have lost, but I wasn't sorry I ran. It was worth the effort and expense because I learned so much. What would I have gained by *not* trying?

I learned that democracy is worth the effort. Trying to be heard, standing up for what you believe, is worth the effort despite the outcome. As that great philosopher/hockey player Wayne Gretzky said, "One hundred percent of the shots you *don't* take won't go in!"

Democracy is about participation, not about winning and losing. Even though I met deceitful and self-serving people in my brief life in politics, I met many good people with good intentions. My work with Heart to Heart has shown me that there are many people in government who truly want to serve others.

Life is not measured by failures and victories. It's measured by attempts and journeys. Thomas Edison tried for a long time to figure out how to make a successful light bulb. It took him years and many failed attempts. But he didn't see the failed attempts as failures. "I have not failed," he said. "I just found 10,000 ways that didn't work!"[3] The light bulb's invention was a process that involved a lot of steps.

This is true when we attempt anything, especially serving others. At Heart to Heart we have tried many different kinds of programs, including a food grains bank that would work as a co-op for hungry regions around the world and a homeless services program, among dozens of others. They didn't all work out. In fact, a lot of them didn't work out, but I don't see them as failures. They were worth the risk and the expense because they helped clarify what we do well and what we don't.

Heart to Heart connects volunteers to people who need them, both locally and abroad, primarily through distribution of medicine and medical supplies. That's what we do best. It took some unsuccessful efforts to find this out.

Robert F. Kennedy said "Only those who dare to fail greatly can ever achieve greatly."[4] Running for Congress was a great risk to me, both personally and financially. I did what I felt I should do, despite the outcome. It put me on a journey for which I am grateful.

As if to put an exclamation point on my unsuccessful bid for Congress, shortly after the primary I was ordered to report to my Army Reserve unit, and within weeks was in a hospital in Kosovo, which led to my meeting the Shabiu family. It became clear I was much better suited to working in medicine to relieve suffering.

Filmmaker Woody Allen said, "If you're not failing every now and again, it's a sign you're not doing anything very innovative."[5]

Success is in the trying, not the outcome. When we serve others, it is useful to go beyond our routine to see what might happen. If we only went with the sure thing, nothing new would ever happen. We have to be willing to "fail" now and then.

Unexpected outcomes can lead to a clearer sense of purpose. This happened with the first airlift we tried to do in China. We had the medicine to fill a cargo plane. we just couldn't get a plane. All of our previous success getting into remote regions meant nothing. We failed to deliver the medicine. But the failure suggested a new idea. What if we took medical *personnel* into China, instead of medicine?

We teamed up with some medical associations to do medical education in China. We trained Chinese doctors in modern surgical procedures in ophthalmology, and they trained us in their traditional medicine. We came back the next year and did training in neonatal resuscitation. More than 40,000 lives were touched because Chinese doctors were able to utilize the methods we taught them.

These were not babies whose lives were *saved*. These were babies born with challenges that would have made it impossible for them to live with their families. They were destined to live in institutions because of cerebral palsy and other severe physical disabilities. All of the medicine we could have loaded onto an airplane would not have saved 40,000 lives. We had to adjust our methods of trying to serve others because our original plan didn't work—but because of this "failure," something better happened.

Now we have FedEx planes going into China with our medicines, and we are still taking medical teams. Our training in emergency medicine went so well that Chinese hospitals are preparing to use it for the Olympic Games when they are held in Beijing.

Failure is what you decide it is. Sometimes it is a launching pad to something better. Losses won't always become victories. But they are part of the effort, part of the journey. Just ask the Boston Red Sox baseball team and their fans! They waited from 1918 until 2004 to finally beat their arch-rival New York Yankees and go on to win the World Series! That's a lot of losing!

Howard Cutler, in his book with the Dalai Lama, *The Art of Happiness*, told of Joseph, one of his clients who had become a multimillionaire during the construction boom in Arizona. Then, in the 1980s, came the biggest real estate crash in Arizona's history. The client, Joseph, lost everything and declared bankruptcy. This put pressure on his marriage, and after twenty-five years of being married Joseph was divorced. He began drinking heavily, but was eventually able to quit with the help of Alcoholics Anonymous. Part of the treatment was for him to become a sponsor to help other alcoholics stay sober.

Joseph realized that he liked helping others. He began using his business knowledge to help people and organizations that were struggling financially. Joseph told Cutler that, despite going from a very rich man to a man of modest means who runs a remodeling business, "I don't really want that kind of money again. I much prefer spending my time volunteering for different groups, working directly with people, helping them out the best I can. These days, I get more pure enjoyment out of one day than I did in a month when I was making the big money. I'm happier than I've ever been in my life!"[6]

Charles Colson is one of the best examples of someone who had to change his way of looking at failing and succeeding. His participation in the Watergate scandal landed him in jail, and led to the resignation of his boss, President Richard Nixon. During a television program that looked back on Watergate, veteran newsman Mike Wallace said to Colson, "Chuck, how do you now look back on Watergate?"

Colson said that his answer had Wallace scratching his head for some time.

"Mike, I thank God for Watergate," Colson said. Wallace looked at Colson with a startled expression.

"Through Watergate I learned the greatest lessons of my life," Colson continued. "The teaching of Jesus is true when he said, 'He who seeks to save his life will lose it. He who loses his life for my sake will find it.'"

Colson's quest for meaning and significance in life began as a child during the Depression, when he saw hungry people standing in lines waiting for bread. "The most important thing would be if I could ever go to college," he thought to himself. No one in his family had gone to college. "I had that great sense of wanting security and wanting to find my meaning, my purpose in life, wanting to get a good education and a good job," he said.

He went to Brown University on a scholarship and, upon graduation, joined the U.S. Marine Corps to fight in the Korean War. When he put his uniform on, he remembered thinking "This is my meaning. My security is as a Marine officer."

After the war he went to law school, and recalled thinking "I'll find my security, my meaning, and my purpose as an attorney."

Colson started a law firm, which grew quickly and made him very successful. He entered politics and became the youngest administrative assistant in the U.S. Senate. He reassured himself "I'll find my meaning and purpose in law and politics." By age 39 he was special counsel to the president of the United States, with an office immediately next door to the president.

When Nixon was re-elected in 1972, Colson said it was time to go back into private practice. "I figured I was a little burned out," he said. "I had a beeper that went off at all times, a telephone beside my bed, the president calling at all hours, crises day and night. I decided that was why I felt so tired and empty inside."

While in prison for his role in the Watergate coverup, Colson had a spiritual awakening that allowed him to identify with Russian writer Alexander Solzhenitsyn, who wrote from a Soviet gulag: "Bless you, prison. Bless you for being in my life. For there, lying on the rotting prison straw, I came to realize that the object of life is not prosperity as we are made to believe, but the maturing of the soul."

"The maturing of the soul," Colson said, "is the object of life."[7]

The way Colson's soul matured out of this "loss" was to begin serving others. His Prison Fellowship organization has changed thousands of prisoners' lives and contributed to significant prison reform around the world.

His early success isn't the success Colson points to now. His education, military status, position, and access to power weren't what ultimately gave him meaning. It was a failure that became meaningful when he began to serve others instead of himself.

Tom and Dana Larson, Howard Cutler's client Joseph, Charles Colson, and I have something in common. We all tried something and it turned out different from our expectations. Some would say we have failed.

But did we? When the loss becomes something that points us to serving others, that's a journey for which we can rejoice.

In *The Art of Happiness*, the authors write that behaviors like serving others despite the circumstances can actually change us from the outside in.

"Just going through the motions and repeatedly engaging in a positive behavior can eventually bring about genuine internal change," they write. This has significant implications for the way we look at failure.

"If we begin with the simple act of regularly helping others, for instance, even if we don't *feel* particularly kind or caring, we may discover an inner transformation is taking place, as we very gradually develop genuine feelings of compassion," they write.[8]

Losing our expectations for a specific outcome, then, isn't a loss at all. Serving others won't have predictable outcomes. We'll find our meaning in unexpected places. Tom and Dana Larson initially "failed" in the Dominican Republic.

But the Dominicans win every time they need a safe drink of water.

CHAPTER EIGHT

LOVE ANYWAY

Love your enemies.
                    Jesus of Nazareth[1]

Watching the news about the U.S. war in Iraq, I became resigned to the fact that I would get the inevitable phone call, as happened during the war in Kosovo. It came in January 2004: "Sir, we've received orders on you, and you're being sent to Iraq."

Because I had expected to get called up, I'd been meeting with the folks at Heart to Heart and also with Docs Who Care, a medical group that provides emergency room doctors to small, under-served communities. Even though I knew the order was coming, the two weeks' notice certainly helped get my priorities in order!

Pre-mobilization occurred at Fort Bliss, Texas, and included anthrax and smallpox vaccinations, weapons practice, briefings, equipment procurement (including a gas mask and chemical protective suit), a new ID card containing DNA samples for identification, and tons of paperwork.

With mixed emotions, I headed for Iraq. When I was deployed as an Army Reserve doctor to Kosovo, NATO bombings had brought the hostilities between the Albanians and the Serbs to a standstill. Things remained tense, but the war was not raging as it was in Iraq. I shed many tears as I said goodbye to my wife and children, my family and friends, my church and the terrific people with whom I work. But, while my heart was heavy, it was also full of love and life and peace and purpose. To be honest, I felt excited and enthusiastic.

I believe that everything we do in life and everything that happens to us is part of a bigger story. My going to Iraq was part of that story. The night before our departure from Fort Bliss, I drove around the little nearby town and heard church bells ringing. It was a small Catholic Church. I went in and sat in the back row. The text was 1 Corinthians 13, the well-known chapter on love. It ends with these words: "We have three things to do: Trust steadily in God, hope unswervingly, love extravagantly. And the best of the three is love." That would be my mission in Iraq.

No matter what else I would be called upon to do there, I wanted to love every person I met or served, whether a wounded American soldier, an Iraqi prisoner, or an innocent civilian. Whatever we might think about this war, surely we can agree that everything we do in this conflict must flow from a loving heart.

My church experience allowed me to have a profound sense of peace as I went forth, and reminded me to love all the people, all the time.

One of the chaplains held a communion service for several dozen of us in a corner of the terminal before we boarded the plane. We arrived in the blazing sunlight of Kuwait about twenty-four hours later, and the next morning I was on a flight to Baghdad. Heart to Heart was able to send along thousands of dollars' worth of donated antibiotics for the local clinics.

My assignment was to be the field doctor for a battalion near the Iranian border, heading a medical team that included a physician's assistant and five medics. My normal duties were to care for soldiers in the medical tent, provide supervision and training to the medics, and visit two camps to care for prisoners. None of it was routine. We worked seven days a week in shifts of twelve to fifteen hours each day. To help distinguish one day from another, the days became known for the unique thing that happened—laundry day, chapel day, and so on.

We were kept busy treating soldiers who had been wounded in firefights, attacks on their convoys, and other violent exchanges. Many died. Our camp was well fortified and protected, so we were never attacked and we slept well. Nearby camps like ours were attacked, with devastating results.

Occasionally I provided medical backup for a mission with the soldiers. One such mission was a surprise sweep in the middle of the night; a group of tanks, mortar platoons, and assault soldiers went to a village suspected of harboring the men who had attacked a nearby military base. When we got close to the village, we extinguished our lights and used night-vision goggles to navigate. Following a detailed plan, each team of soldiers knew which houses to search and in which order to search them. It happened quickly, quietly, smoothly. Within two hours the sweep was complete, the soldiers having apprehended two men hiding with an enormous cache of weapons. There were no more attacks on our bases in that area.

One of the Iraqi detainees developed a severe abdominal infection, which we tried to treat at the field hospital. But he was in worse shape than we could handle, so we requested transport to take him to the military hospital in Baghdad. In wartime, there is no routine transport. On the road everything is a potential target, and this transport meant organizing a convoy of vehicles involving dozens of soldiers. Without the convoy, this man would die. The convoy was immediately approved.

On the day we were scheduled to go, however, the mission was scrapped. The convoy coming to our camp the night before had been hit by a bomb. It was the third time in five days that one of our convoys had been hit, so we waited until a nearby combat unit could beef up security. A day later we were able to head out.

As I sat in the back of a Humvee with this very sick Iraqi prisoner of war, I asked myself the question that every soldier in that convoy was probably asking: Why are we doing this for someone we consider our enemy? It seemed unfair. I could see risking the lives of Americans for another American. But for an enemy?

I felt very lonely and homesick. There I was in an armored vehicle, wearing fifty pounds of body armor, helmet, weapon— full "battle rattle"—and standing next to me was the machine gunner, constantly spinning, looking for snipers, motioning for vehicles to move out of the way and screaming at drivers who didn't respond. We drove as fast as we could, Humvees tailgating one another to present a more difficult target and to prevent a suicide-bomb–rigged car from getting between us. In front was a soldier monitoring the radio, relaying messages from the Humvees ahead of us to the gunner and me.

Feeling sorry for myself, I took out my MP3 player. Soldiers need to be alert and vigilant, but I thought "What's the big deal? I'm the senior officer on this convoy, and no one is going to say anything to me about it." So I poked the earphones under my helmet and into my ears, and turned on the music.

My son-in-law, Eric, had loaded my player with about a thousand songs. Since it was Sunday, I decided to listen to the first religious song I came to. It was the Brooklyn Tabernacle Choir singing Lanny Wolfe's "Surely the Presence of the Lord Is in This Place." I had heard Wolfe's song hundreds of times before, but on that day, in that place, the words were a potent reminder for me.

Speeding toward Baghdad, crammed into the back of a Humvee, with many lives in the balance, I sensed the presence of God as never before. I literally felt enveloped by God: God around me, God above me, God in me.

Tears running down my dusty cheeks, I peered through the thick bullet-proof window at Iraqis in their native dress, at their mud-walled houses, at children playing, at the tall and stately palm trees. And, just as surely as I felt the presence of God in that Humvee, I sensed God's presence in all that I looked upon here, in this desolate country, with the Shiites, the Sunnis, and the Kurds.

God loves Iraq.

Then I thought of what this convoy was doing, and the words of Jesus came to me: "Greater love has no man than this, that he be willing to lay down his life for another." I was filled with a deep sense of peace. I was still worried about the road ahead, but I had a sense that everything was going to be fine, no matter what happened. I was proud of every gunner and driver in every one of the Humvees that day. They were putting their lives at risk to do something honorable and noble and sacred. And I knew that God profoundly loves every person on both sides of this war.

This sense of peace and contentment lasted throughout my time in Iraq. It had nothing to do with bravery or courage. I was able to find an oasis from the danger every now and then in a secluded place at the edge of the camp, amid some beautiful wildflowers. It was there that I read these words from the Bible: "Don't fret or worry. Instead of worrying, pray. Let petitions and praises shape your worries into prayers, letting God know your concerns. Before you know it, a sense of God's wholeness, everything coming together for good, will come and settle you down. It's wonderful when Christ displaces worry at the center of your life. I've learned by now to be quite content whatever my circumstances. . . . Whatever I have, wherever I am, I can make it through anything in the One who makes me who I am."[2]

My time in Iraq ended a few weeks early when our medical team responded to a serious car accident on the highway. Since it was outside the camp, we were required to wear full battle gear. There was some concern that this might not be an accident but an ambush, so we were told that a quick reaction force (QRF) team was already on the scene securing the area.

When we got to the accident site, the QRF was not there. We had beaten them to the scene. We had to act fast, since we were in enemy territory with only a couple of soldiers to protect us. It was pitch black and as the ambulance rolled to a stop we opened the back doors and jumped out. My 52-year-old left knee, which I had injured in college thirty years before, couldn't handle the jump with all of the extra gear. It just gave out. We cared for the accident victims and got back to the camp safely. I figured that I had just twisted my knee and it would get better on its own.

A few days later, as I was working in the emergency room in Baghdad, one of the orthopedic doctors saw me limping and insisted on examining my knee. He said I had torn the cartilage and needed to have it repaired as soon as possible. So I went to Iraq as a doctor and left as a patient. Within a few days I was on a MEDEVAC flight to Germany, then flown to San Antonio, Texas, for knee surgery.

Before I left, I met with military officials to discuss my returning on a Heart To Heart mission with aid for the Iraqis. The officials were responsive, partly because some remembered what happened after my time in Kosovo, and they have developed respect for humanitarian missions.

The Saturday before I left was one of the most amazing days of my life. I was scheduled to see patients and make rounds at the prisoner camp. One of the Iraqi prisoners pulled me aside when I was finished, telling me it was an Iraqi tradition to give a good friend a gift. He stunned me by slowly slipping his wedding band off: "This is my wedding ring. I haven't seen my wife in many years, and I probably will never see her again. I'd like to give it to you."

Speechless at first, I finally replied "No, you need to keep this. Your wife will want you to have it—I think you'll see her again. You'll find her."

What he told me has haunted me. He said he didn't think he would live long enough to see her. He felt that he would be killed very soon. We hugged and said a tearful goodbye, and then I walked out of the POW compound.

I can debate the war with anyone, now that I have seen it firsthand. For me, personally, my purpose was to serve—despite the debate—ally and enemy alike. I was brought up in a home where my parents read the Bible. As a child it was perplexing to hear the words "Love your enemy." How is that possible?

The writer Wendell Berry describes this same tension in his novel *Jayber Crow*. The narrator describes his frustration as his small town prepared to go to war during World War II. The narrator had been raised with "Love your enemy," as I had been.

"Did I think that the great organizations of the world could love their enemies? I did not," he wrote. "I didn't think great organizations could love anything."

The narrator asked, What caused this war?

"It was caused, I thought, by people failing to love one another, failing to love their enemies. I was glad enough that I had not become a preacher, and so would not have to go through a war pretending that Jesus had not told us to love our enemies."[3]

I just cannot escape those words: Love your enemy. I don't understand them. I resist them. But if our lives are going to be committed to serving others, some of those "others" will be our enemy.

The words of Jesus are paraphrased this way in a book called *The Message*: "Give away your life. . . . What you have is all you'll ever get. And it's trouble ahead if you're satisfied with yourself. Your self will not satisfy you for long. Life is not about *us*. It's not a popularity contest. Our task is to be true, not popular. Love your enemies. Let them bring out the best in you. It's an opportunity, so use the occasion to live the servant life. If you only love the lovable, do you expect a medal? Live generously. Generosity begets generosity."[4]

I would add the following: You can *make a living*, which is to measure what you get—or you can *have a life*, which is to measure what you give.

The concept of loving enemies becomes a little easier, I believe, when we take seriously that "Life is not about us." When we begin to get the message that we are *not* the center of the universe, we can begin to get over ourselves. Seeing enemies and loving them is a measure of how well we are doing.

Anne Lamott writes about the difficulty she had with this concept, especially when she realized it was non-negotiable.

"It meant trying to respect them," she said, of those she considered her enemies. "It meant identifying with their humanity and weaknesses. It didn't mean unconditional acceptance of their crazy behavior. They were still accountable for the atrocities they'd perpetrated, as you were accountable for yours. But you worked at doing better, at loving them, for the profoundest spiritual reason: You were trying not to make things worse."[5]

When Adolph Coors IV was a boy growing up in Colorado, an escaped prisoner ambushed his father on his way to work early one morning. Seven months later his father's remains were found near a dump site, forty miles away. The young boy's mother was despondent and turned to alcohol. Adolph eventually joined the Marines and became obsessed with muscles and power. When he got out of the Marines, his obsession turned to money and power, just a minor tweak of the original obsession.

After a near-fatal car accident and a realization that his marriage was failing, Coors had a conversion experience and came to a similar conclusion as the angel in the Tolstoy story: He saw that living for others was the key to a happy life. But there was one aspect of his life that still plagued him. He desperately hated the man who killed his father.

The man had been captured in Canada and sentenced to life in prison in Colorado.

"I hated the man," Coors said. "But hatred is like a treacherous acid, which cannot be poured without spilling on the raw heart that holds it. I can speak from experience that hate hurts the hater far more than the person being hated."

With help from others, Coors eventually went to the prison to see his father's killer. The prisoner refused to see him. Three separate times he refused. So Coors sent him a letter, asking him to forgive the hatred he had harbored for so many years. Coors added that he forgave the man for the pain and suffering he had caused the Coors family. The hatred in Coors' heart was replaced with love.[6]

How can this be?

It's about being changed from the outside in. As we reach out to address needs of others, our own lives are changed dramatically. "Within the context of action one experiences the mystical presence of God," said sociologist Tony Campolo.[7] This is what I mean when I say "Love anyway." When we begin to *act as if* we love, whether we feel like it or not, we begin to truly love.

"Maybe you don't have to love your enemies," said Jayber Crow. "Maybe you just have to act like you do. And maybe you have to start early."[8]

Loving enemies, or loving and acting despite the circumstances, involves a decision on our part. Many people don't do it simply because they don't know it is an option. Or they think it would be too difficult. But everything is too difficult if we only *think* about doing it. Things become much simpler when we *decide* to try something, and then actually try it. We can start where we are.

This kind of action requires a decision that, over time, becomes easier to make. The Dalai Lama tells of a Tibetan Buddhist monk who had been in Chinese prisons as a political prisoner and in labor camps for twenty years. "Once I asked him what was the most difficult situation he faced in prison," the Dalai Lama said. "Surprisingly, he said that he felt the greatest danger was of losing compassion for the Chinese."[9]

In a different Tolstoy story from that cited in the Introduction, one called "Master and Man," the main character, a greedy merchant named Brekhunoff, and his hired hand, a simpleton named Nikita, head for a village in a brutal snowstorm. Brekhunoff leaves the sled with Nikita in it and, concerned only with himself, tries to go through the storm alone on the horse. Unable to make any progress, he returns to the sled, where Nikita has nearly frozen to death. At first Brekhunoff tries to protect the servant as he would any of his property. But in the act of offering his warm body to the peasant, and feeling Nikita revive, Brekhunoff is transformed.

"Then he began to think about his money, his store, his house, his sales and purchases, and [his competitor's] millions," Tolstoy wrote. "He could not understand how that man whom men called Vassili Brekhunoff could bear to interest himself in such things as he did." Life for Brekhunoff had been measured in what he could acquire. But as he gives himself in service to Nikita, he is fulfilled.[10]

The decision to love others, particularly adversaries, came to Bud Anderson in Auburn, California, several years ago when a drunk driver crashed into the car carrying the entire Anderson family on their way to church one Sunday morning. Bud held his injured son in the street, unaware that the 10-year-old boy had already died. A 6-year-old daughter died en route to the hospital. Two other children were seriously injured. The scene on the road was so gruesome that the first Highway Patrol officer to arrive took a look in the car and drove away to direct traffic instead. He resigned from the force the next day.

"Dad's sorrow was overwhelming," said Ted Anderson, one of the children who was injured, who is now a university professor. "How do you go on after that?"

Two things helped prevent the Anderson family from feeling bitterness and malice toward the drunk driver who killed two of their children. One was a verse from the Bible that Bud had read all his life: "Love your enemies." The other was that Bud discovered that the driver had a family, a wife and two teenagers, and they had fallen on hard times. The man had recently lost his job and was about to lose the family's trailer home as well.

His predicament moved Bud to visit the man in jail.

"I told him I wasn't going to hurt him or his family," Bud said. "I told him I forgave him. He was dumbfounded."

At the sentencing, the judge asked Anderson what he believed the punishment should be.

"I said 'Nothing you do could bring my children back, so instead of tearing his family apart, and leaving two families with significant losses, I think we should help him.'"

The judge sentenced the man to six months of *weekends* in jail so he could find a new job and support his family.

"We could not have done that without the right spirit," Anderson said. "One man who stopped at the accident site told me that if this had happened to his family he would have killed the drunk driver right there in the street. The love of God keeps you from reacting that way."

Examples like this make me think that, maybe, with practice and with the desire, it is truly possible to love one's enemy.

When the apartheid system collapsed in South Africa, the Truth and Reconciliation Commission was charged with reconciling blacks and whites. They were to bring about justice and determine punishment. John Roth, in his book *Choosing Against War*, describes an elderly black woman whose son had been shot by white police officers, who then set the boy's body on fire and celebrated around it. Years later, the same men took her husband and set him on fire, after tying him to a pile of wood and dousing him with gasoline.

The commission had her face the leader of the group, a man named Van de Broek, as it prepared to sentence him. The men had confessed their guilt, and the commission asked the woman what she considered an appropriate punishment.

"I want three things," she said. "I want Mr. Van de Broek to take me to the place where they burned my husband's body. I would like to gather up the dust and give him a decent burial.

"Second, Mr. Van de Broek took all my family away from me, and I still have a lot to give. Twice a month, I would like him to come to the ghetto and spend the day with me so I can be a mother to him.

"Third, I would like Mr. Van de Broek to know he is forgiven by God and that I forgive him too. And, I would like someone to come and lead me by the hand to where Mr. Van de Broek is so that I can embrace him and he can know my forgiveness is real."[11]

I'll be the first to admit that this kind of response is uncommon. It doesn't seem humanly possible. But many of us don't even think of this kind of action as an alternative. Not only is it an alternative, it is a way of acting that takes us out of living for ourselves and into living for others.

In the book *Father Joe*, writer Tony Hendra discusses this paradox with his mentor, who tells Hendra "True courage is not to hate our enemy, any more than to fight and kill him. To love him, to love in the teeth of his hate—that is real bravery. That ought to earn people medals."[12]

This kind of behavior isn't rewarded by medals or salaries or elected office. But it can change our lives, and our world.

Anyway: The Paradoxical Commandments was written by Kent Keith. A copy of his commandments hangs in a prominent place in one of Mother Teresa's orphanages in Calcutta:

People are illogical, unreasonable and self-centered.
Love them anyway.

If you do good, people will accuse you of
selfish ulterior motives.
Do good anyway.

If you are successful, you will win false friends
and true enemies.
Succeed anyway.

The good you do today will be forgotten tomorrow.
Do good anyway.

Honesty and frankness make you vulnerable.
Be honest and frank anyway.

The biggest men and women with the biggest ideas
can be shot down by the smallest men and women with
the smallest minds.
Think big anyway.

People favor underdogs but follow only top dogs.
Fight for a few underdogs anyway.

What you spend years building may be destroyed overnight.
Build anyway.

People really need help but may attack you if you
do help them.
Help people anyway.

Give the world the best you have and you'll
get kicked in the teeth.
Give the world the best you have anyway. [13]

Keith says that these commandments focus on something other than what the culture seems to value (celebrity, influence, money). Instead, the focus is on helping, loving, improving, persevering, looking out for those who can't look out for themselves. It is a change in focus, he claims, from looking inward to looking outside of ourselves. When we make a difference in the lives of others, he says, we make our own lives different—for the better. [14]

Helping others see that it is possible to live this way is one of the great favors we can do for people around us. Psychiatrist Scott Peck, the well-known author, told of a woman patient who was suffering from extreme depression. She called him on the day of her appointment to tell him she wouldn't be able to make it because her car had broken down. Peck told her he was willing to pick her up if she didn't mind waiting in the car while he briefly visited a couple of patients in a nearby hospital.

When they got to the hospital, Peck had an inspiration. He suggested that the woman make his hospital calls. An hour and a half later the woman returned to the car in a buoyant mood. She said trying to cheer up those two patients had lifted her own spirits and she felt wonderful.

Peck said to her: "Now we know how to get you out of your depression. Now we know the cure for your problem."

To which the woman replied, "You don't expect me to do that every day, do you?"[15]

I had the option of letting the enemy Iraqi die from his abdominal infection. Adolph Coors IV had the option of continuing to hate his father's killer. Bud Anderson had the option of bitterly arguing for a lengthy prison sentence for his children's killer. The South African woman had the option of asking that her family's killers be locked away forever.

These are legitimate options, and similar ones are exercised every day by people around the world. If we are serious about finding meaning and significance in our lives, though, there *are* other options. They include loving, forgiving, and serving. By choosing them we will come to know what we were put on this earth to do.

When I revisited the Shabiu family in Kosovo as a civilian, a couple of years had passed since their daughter Merita was murdered. After being with them most of the day, I asked how they felt about

Merita's killer, who is serving a sentence of life without parole in a United States federal penitentiary.

"Do you have a message you would like me to take to him when I return to the United States?" I asked. Merita's parents discussed my question in their native Albanian language for several minutes.

Then I asked a different question.

"Do you think he should be killed for what he did to your daughter?"

More discussion.

Finally Merita's father said "He is already paying the price for his actions. We don't see the purpose of two mothers weeping. One is enough."

That's loving anyway.

CHAPTER NINE

PULL OUT THE ARROW

*If one comes across a person who has been
shot by an arrow, one does not spend time
wondering about where the arrow came from,
or the caste of the individual who shot it, or
analyzing what type of wood the shaft is made
of, or the manner in which the arrowhead
was fashioned. Rather, one should focus on
immediately pulling out the arrow.*

Shakyamuni, the Buddha[1]

One of my favorite places to practice medicine is in the high
mountains of Papua, New Guinea, among the most ancient
civilizations in the world. It is a population that was discovered by
planes flying over the mountains during World War II. Every few
years I get to visit their clinics, which have none of the conveniences
of modern hospitals.

Some of the villages where I work take days to reach. A small
plane deposits me on a rudimentary airstrip, and then it's another
one or two days' hike into the jungle to reach the hospital. The tribes
in these jungles have been at war with one another for thousands of
years. And, while some of the villages have electricity and cars, they
still settle their tribal differences with their weapon of choice: the
bow and arrow.

Many of the injuries the hospitals treat involve warriors coming
in with arrows sticking out of their chests. I have never asked, nor
have I heard anyone on the medical staff ask, "Who shot you?" None
of us has ever commented on the high quality of the arrow. Nor have
we asked the victim, "What did you do to deserve this?" We have
never said, "Can't you find a more humane way to disagree?"

Our job is to pull out the arrow.

This is something each of us can do for the people around us. Someone within your reach is grieving the loss of a loved one. That's an arrow we can pull out by visiting with that person and offering to help. Someone within your reach is having difficulty getting to the bus stop. You can pull out that arrow by giving the person a ride. Someone is having difficulty finding a babysitter, or the money for a tank of gas, or a meal. Arrows. They are sticking out of people all around us, if we would only see them. It's a matter of seeing and doing.

Everyone can do something.

Much of this book has been about changing the way we look at the world and our roles in it. Instead of seeing a world full of need and saying "I am overwhelmed by this," we can see a world full of need and say "I can do something about this. I have something someone needs. I can help."

Malcolm Gladwell, in his book *The Tipping Point*, said that dimensions of the world that seem so concrete (for instance, the belief that I have nothing to offer that could improve the world) can change when people see that change is possible, and that they can change their behavior and beliefs with the right kind of catalyst.

"Look at the world around you," he writes. "It may seem like an immovable, implacable place. It is not. With the slightest push in just the right place it can be tipped."[2]

In this book I have tried to show how natural it is for us to serve each other. It comes at a cost of money, time, and attention, but I hope by now readers can see that all of us have something to give, right now, that will help someone. In doing so, we address one of life's fundamental questions, the one that was raised by the angel in Tolstoy's story who asked "What do we live by?" What gives our lives purpose and meaning? Love for each other, taking care of each other, serving each other, that's what we live by.

Most people are willing to give when they see the need. Everyone can do something right now.

Madeleine L'Engle, one of the great children's writers, tells of being interviewed by a Columbia University student. In answer to a question, L'Engle said that she does "small things which are daily put into my path to do, such as smiling at the dour man trying to deliver those boxes of groceries down the metal slide." The student asked if that were self-serving.

"Is it?" L'Engle asks. "It may be, but if I cannot see the hungry people I pass each day, if I do not smile at the dour man, if I do not feed the stranger who comes to my door, or give a glass of cool water to the thirsty child, then I cannot see the starvation of people in India or South America. Perhaps if I see pictures on the news or in the papers of victims of earthquake, flood, or drought, I will write a small check for the cause of world hunger, and I may even refrain from meat on Wednesdays; but as long as I am responding to a cause it will not affect my entire life, my very breathing. It is only when I see hunger or thirst in one human being, it is only when I see discrimination and injustice in all its horrendous particularity as I walk along Broadway, that my very life can be changed."[3]

She captures the essence of what it means to serve others. It isn't about joining a cause, or starting a new relief effort. L'Engel sees that there are needs all around us every day, and we have the opportunity to meet those needs. That's how we serve and love. That's what we live by. There is an arrow within reach.

An elderly woman in my church, Mattie Uphaus, showed me the truth of this when, just a few years before she died, she told our congregation about growing up on a small farm in Kansas. At Christmas one year, the pastor of her little community church told about a family in the congregation that had very little—the children had barely enough to eat or wear, and certainly had no toys or money. His plea to the members was to make that family's Christmas special.

As a little girl, Mattie discussed the plight of this poor family with her parents and siblings, and they committed to collecting some of their own money for these unfortunate people.

They each sacrificed some coins when they could, and at the church service where the collection occurred, Mattie and her family proudly went to the front to deposit about $2.

When it came time for the gifts to be delivered, Mattie said she got the shock of her life. It was *her* family the minister had been describing! It was for *her* family that the church had collected money.

"Apparently we were that poor and I didn't know it!" she said to our laughing congregation. "And it was quite a letdown. The joy for us was in conspiring to give. It wasn't nearly as much fun to receive." What struck me about her story was the response of her family members when they first heard about this "poor" family. They knew they could give something. Everyone has something to give. We can all start where we are.

Something happens to us when we begin to live in service to others. Our lives make more sense. When Mitch Albom began visiting his dying professor, Morrie Schwartz, Mitch wrote "I liked myself better when I was there."[4] He liked himself better because he realized that this is what we are put on this earth to do. Morrie taught Mitch some valuable lessons, especially through some of the last words Morrie uttered on earth: "Love each other or die."[5]

By visiting Morrie, by bringing him groceries each Tuesday, by simply listening to him, Mitch served Morrie, and Mitch discovered the power and purpose in that action. He gave his world a push in the right direction, as Gladwell would say, and his world changed for the better.

Something else happens when we serve others. I believe that when we look to others' needs, we can experience a transcendence that connects us to a far bigger world. Rabbi Lawrence Kushner (no relation to Harold Kushner) said: "Everyone carries with them at least one and probably many pieces to someone else's puzzle. Sometimes they know it; sometimes they don't know it. And when you present your piece, which is worthless to you, to another, whether you know it or not, whether they know it or not, you are a messenger from the Most High."[6]

By pulling out the arrow, by serving others, by loving others, we provide a piece to life's puzzle that everyone is searching for. We help someone and discover there is power in doing so— power to live as we were meant to live. That's what Mother Teresa discovered when she began serving the poorest of the poor. It's what Pete O'Neal discovered when he and Charlotte began serving their community. It's what the Larsons discovered when they began providing water to their village. It's what Mattie Uphaus discovered when she sacrificed for that "poor" family.

In a commencement address to university students, Anne Lamott gave graduates the following advice: "First, find a path and a little light to see by. Then push up your sleeves and start helping. Every single spiritual tradition says that you must take care of the poor, or you are so doomed that not even Jesus or the Buddha can help you. You don't have to go overseas. There are people in this country who are poor in spirit, worried, depressed, dancing as fast as they can; their kids are sick, or their retirement savings are gone. There is great loneliness among us, life-threatening loneliness. People have given up on peace, on equality. . . . You do what you can, what good people have always done: you bring thirsty people water, you share your food, you try to help the homeless find shelter, you stand up for the underdog."[7]

We can't wait any longer for government to fill the gaps. We've seen what happens when we leave it to institutions. Handouts aren't the answer. Our presence is the answer. When we leave serving others to government and corporations, we lose the opportunity to find meaning and significance in our own lives.

What can each of us do? Look around you. We are the people others have been waiting for.

Now look in your hand. See that plant on the cover of this book? It's growing. *The power of serving others* starts now.

Right where you are.

HOW WE GOT STARTED

ABOUT HEART TO HEART

The story of Heart to Heart International is all about connecting people and resources to a world in need. Heart to Heart started as an idea to get people in the heart of America involved in helping people in the heart of Russia. The same ideals that motivated Dr. Gary Morsch, Heart to Heart's founder, to organize the largest volunteer airlift in U.S. history still resonate today in all of the organization's humanitarian operations.

One of the great things about that first airlift was that everybody was invited to help in the initiative. People from all walks of life were captivated by the idea that they could be part of something that had a global impact. Heart to Heart continues to invite people to serve their fellowman, whether across the street or around the world. The organization also seeks to help people in desperate need, regardless of their race, religion, or personal or political beliefs.

Volunteers that participated with Heart to Heart's inaugural airlift discovered a significant benefit in serving others. Many of them said that the airlift was one of the most meaningful things they had done in their lives. Today, Heart to Heart offers multiple opportunities for meaningful service. The organization believes that lives are transformed when people who can help connect with people in need. The amazing thing is that both the recipient and the volunteer are changed in the process. Volunteers often say that they received more than they gave through their service experience. This transformation is all part of Heart to Heart's "people agenda."

Though volunteers are an important part of Heart to Heart's vision to create a healthier world, the organization relies heavily on key partnerships to literally get the work off the ground. On that first airlift, Heart to Heart found partners within the pharmaceutical industry, in civic groups, in faith communities, in high government offices, and others. Annually, Heart to Heart assists 250 organizations with over $100 million in humanitarian aid and supplies. This level of assistance has created strong partnerships with major Fortune 500 companies and the largest pharmaceutical companies in the world. Heart to Heart is shaping the culture of these partners by helping them connect to a world in need.

The genius of Heart to Heart's first airlift was that everything was donated: all the medicines and first-aid supplies, the cargo plane, the financial support, and the volunteer hours. Heart to Heart continues that tradition of efficiency, while always striving to deliver the highest quality in each of its humanitarian efforts. The organization is consistently among the leading humanitarian organizations in terms of fiscal responsibility. Historically, Heart to Heart operates on less than 2 percent overhead, meaning that more than 98 percent of all contributions goes directly to humanitarian operations. On average, Heart to Heart is able to leverage each $1 donation to procure and deliver $25 worth of medical aid.

WHAT WE DO

Since 1992, more than $1 billion of aid and supplies have been delivered through Heart to Heart to over 150 countries, including the United States. The organization identifies pockets of human need and finds ways to satisfy those needs. Heart to Heart utilizes volunteers and members of its global alliance to create a viable supply line of medical aid and other services. The primary outcome of Heart to Heart's work is a healthier world. Because of Heart to

Heart's humanitarian programs, millions of people live healthier lives, disaster survivors have hope, newborns take their first breath, people have their sight restored, mothers survive the birthing process, and America's poor and needy know that someone cares about them.

Here is a summary of Heart to Heart's global operations:

- Internationally, Heart to Heart works to improve the quality of medical care and strives to increase access to essential health services in developing countries. The organization recruits volunteers and solicits members of its global alliance to provide medical training to health professionals, advocates policy changes to make health care more affordable and available, organizes special projects aimed at raising the quality of life for vulnerable women and children, and operates effectively within the local infrastructure to create healthier communities. Heart to Heart also functions as experts in humanitarian-assistance programs within the global-response community to address broader issues such as human pandemics, child mortality, and maternal health.

- In the United States, Heart to Heart works to increase the quality of life for some of America's poorest and most vulnerable populations. By training and placing volunteers within its agency support network, Heart to Heart expands the capacity of these institutions to serve the poor in their communities. Further, the organization engages its partners to support local and national initiatives designed to help people live healthier lives. Heart to Heart is one of only a handful of organizations that has vibrant operations both internationally and domestically.

- In times of disaster, Heart to Heart takes a holistic approach. Along with the organization's global alliance, Heart to Heart has created a readiness structure that allows it to respond to victims of natural disaster and human tragedy anywhere in the world. As Heart to Heart mobilizes its volunteer base and alliance members, the organization works to save as many lives as possible by providing frontline medical support, durable shelter, clean drinking water, and nonperishable food items to assist survivors through the first difficult days and weeks following a crisis event. Heart to Heart then works closely with local officials in the recovery effort, so that the communities can begin to think about the future. As the rebuilding process gets underway, Heart to Heart often helps in infrastructure-building projects that focus on clinics, schools, and community centers. The organization's ultimate goal in every crisis response is to help a better and stronger community emerge in the aftermath of a disaster. Because of Heart to Heart's expertise in crisis response, the international relief community often calls upon the organization to lead specific initiatives aimed at restoring medical services and rebuilding lives.

If you are interested in learning more about Heart to Heart, joining its growing force of volunteers, or getting your company or organization involved in its global alliance, contact the organization in one of the following ways:

Heart to Heart International
www.hearttoheart.org
Email: info@hearttoheart.org
Phone: 913-764-5200
Fax: 913-764-0809

NOTES

Introduction

1   Joseph Campbell, *The Power of Myth* (New York: Anchor, 1991), p. xiv.
2   Leo Tolstoy, "What Men Live By," *Walk in the Light & TwentyThree Tales* (Maryknoll, NY: Orbis, 2003), p. 121–44.
3   Sheryl Fred, "Can't Hurry Love," *Science & Spirit* 14(1): 38.
4   His Holiness The Dalai Lama and Howard Cutler, *The Art of Happiness* (New York: Riverhead, 1998), p. 58–59.
5   *Ibid.*, p. 59.
6   *Ibid.*
7   Fred, "Can't Hurry Love," 38.
8   Richard A. Kauffman, "Beyond Bake Sales," *Christianity Today* (June 16, 1997): 12.
9   *Ibid.*, 13.
10 Campbell, *The Power of Myth*, p. 4–5.
11 Fyodor Dostoevsky, *The Brothers Karamazov* (New York: Bantam, 1970), p. 935–36.
12 Huston Smith, *Why Religion Matters* (San Francisco: HarperSanFrancisco, 2001), p. 206.
13 Mitch Albom, *Tuesdays with Morrie* (New York: Doubleday, 1997), p. 43–44.
14 Kauffman, "Beyond Bake Sales," 13.

Chapter 1: Get in the Boat

1   Mitch Albom, *Tuesdays with Morrie* (New York: Doubleday, 1997), p. 163.

Chapter 2: Get Over Yourself

1   William Sloane Coffin, *The Heart is a Little to the Left* (Hanover: University Press of New England, 1999), p. 12.
2   Dostoevsky, *The Brothers Karamazov*, p. 277.
3   John 13:5
4   Jim Wallis, *God's Politics* (San Francisco: HarperSanFrancisco, 2005), p. 16.
5   Henri Nouwen, *Adam* (Maryknoll, New York: Orbis Books, 1997), p. 76.
6   *Ibid.*, p. 90

Chapter 3: Look in Your Hand
1. *Babette's Feast,* Orion Classics, 1987.
2. Frederick Buechner, *The Sacred Journey* (New York: HarperCollins, 1982), p. 107.
3. Anne Lamott, *Traveling Mercies* (New York: Pantheon Books, 1999) p. 68.
4. Henri Nouwen, *Reaching Out* (New York: Doubleday, 1975), p. 9.
5. *Ibid.,* p. 48.

Chapter 4: Give What You Can
1. Tony Hendra, *Father Joe* (New York: Random House, 2004), p. 99.
2. Wendell Berry, *Jayber Crow* (New York: Counterpoint, 2000), pp. 149–150.

Chapter 5: Think Small
1. Anne Lamott, *Plan B* (New York: Riverhead, 2005), p. 132.
2. Luke 10: 30–37.
3. Thomas Keating, *The Kingdom of God Is Like. . .* (New York: Crossroad, 1994), p. 19–21.
4. Harold Kushner, *How Good Do We Have to Be?* (Boston: Little, Brown, 1996), p. 140–41.
5. *Ibid., p.* 63.
6. Huston Smith, *Why Religion Matters* (San Francisco: HarperSanFrancisco, 2001), p. 151–53.

Chapter 6: Be There
1. Harold Kushner, *Living a Life That Matters* (New York: Knopf, 2001), p. 145.
2. Tony Campolo, *Let Me Tell You a Story* (Nashville: Word, 2000), p. 216–20.
3. Anne Lamott, *Traveling Mercies* (New York: Pantheon, 1999), p. 163.
4. Tony Hendra, *Father Joe* (New York: Random House, 2004), p. 95–96.
5. *Ibid.,* p. 269.
6. Henri Nouwen, *Reaching Out* (New York: Doubleday, 1975), p. 46.
7. Lauren Winner, *Mudhouse Sabbath* (Brewster, MA: Paraclete, 2003), p. 40–53.
8. Henri Nouwen, *Reaching Out,* p. 51.
9. *Hotel Rwanda,* film, United Artists, 2004.
10. James Fowler, *Stages of Faith* (San Francisco: HarperSanFrancisco, 1981), p. 203.
11. Harold Kushner, *Living a Life That Matters,* p. 86–97.

Chapter 7: Lose to Win
1. Viktor Frankl, *Man's Search for Meaning* (New York: Washington Square, 1963), p. 24.
2. Robert Pirsig, *Zen and the Art of Motorcycle Maintenance* (New York: Bantam, 1974), p. 273.

3. Quoted by Scott LaFee in "Fail Safe," *The San Diego Union Tribune,* July 20, 2005, F-1.
4. *Ibid.,* F-4.
5. *Ibid.*
6. His Holiness The Dalai Lama and Howard Cutler, *The Art of Happiness* (New York: Riverhead, 1998), p. 127–28.
7 Dwight Johnson, *The Transparent Leader* (Mechanicsburg, PA: Executive Books, 2001), p. 15–23.
8. His Holiness The Dalai Lama and Howard Cutler, *The Art of Happiness,* p. 230–31.

Chapter 8: Love Anyway
1. Matthew 5::44.
2. Philippians 4:6–7, 11–13.
3. Wendell Berry, *Jayber Crow* (New York: Counterpoint, 2000), p. 142–143.
4. Eugene Peterson, *The Message* (Colorado Springs: Navpress, 1993), p. 21–22.
5. Anne Lamott, *Plan B* (New York: Riverhead, 2005), p. 225.
6. Dwight Johnson, *The Transparent Leader* (Mechanicsburg, PA: Executive Books, 2001), p. 76–86.
7. Gary Morsch and Dean Nelson, *Heart and Soul* (Kansas City: Beacon Hill, 1997), p. 11.
8. Wendell Berry, *Jayber Crow,* p. 142.
9. His Holiness The Dalai Lama and Howard Cutler, *The Art of Happiness* (New York: Riverhead, 1998), p. 302.
10 Leo Tolstoy, *Great Short Works of Leo Tolstoy* (New York: HarperCollins, 1967), p. 451–500.
11. Philip Gulley and James Mulholland, *If God Is Love* (San Francisco: HarperSanFrancisco, 2004), p. 265–66.
12. Tony Hendra, *Father Joe* (New York: Random House, 2004), p. 118.
13. Kent Keith, *Anyway: The Paradoxical Commandments* (New York: Putnam, 2001), p. 105–107.
14. *Ibid.*
15. Tony Campolo, *Let Me Tell You a Story* (Nashville: Word, 2000), p. 91.

Chapter 9: Pull Out the Arrow
1. His Holiness The Dalai Lama and Howard Cutler, *The Art of Happiness* (New York: Riverhead, 1998), p. 246.
2. Malcolm Gladwell, *The Tipping Point* (Boston: Little, Brown, 2000), p. 259.
3. Madeleine L'Engle, *The Irrational Season* (New York; Crosswicks, 1977), p. 139.
4. Mitch Albom, *Tuesdays with Morrie* (New York: Doubleday, 1997), p. 55.
5. *Ibid.,* p. 163.
6. Harold Kushner, *Living a Life That Matters* (New York: Knopf, 2001), p. 143.
7. Anne Lamott, *Plan B* (New York: Riverhead, 2005), pp. 307–308.

ABOUT THE AUTHORS

Gary Morsch, MD, is the founder and president of Heart to Heart International, a global humanitarian assistance organization dedicated to improving health and alleviating human suffering throughout the world. Since 1992 this grassroots organization has delivered nearly $1 billion in pharmaceuticals and medical supplies to people in need in over 150 countries. Morsch believes that every individual is uniquely gifted and called to serve others. His life-long commitment to volunteerism has taken him literally around the world—from inner-city shelters to rural clinics, from refugee camps to mission hospitals, providing crisis evaluation and organizing programs to meet the needs of the poor.

A family physician, Dr. Morsch serves Heart to Heart as a volunteer but continues to practice medicine with Docs Who Care, Inc., a medical staffing company he founded. Morsch has received numerous awards, including the President's Volunteer Action Award, the Points of Light Community Leadership Award, the International Relations Council Community Service Award, the Salvation Army's Others Award, the Washington Times Foundation National Service Award, and the first-ever Humanitarian Award offered by the American Academy of Family Physicians.

Morsch has written several books. His book with co-author Dean Nelson, *The Power of Serving Others*, shares the amazing story of Heart to Heart and introduces the reader to people whose lives have been transformed by the extraordinary power released when we respond to the needs of our fellow men and women.

Morsch served 21 years in the U.S Active Army and U.S. Army Reserve, where he retired as Colonel in 2012.

Gary Morsch and his wife, Vickie, a former school nurse, are the parents of four children and have 8 grandchildren. They reside on a small farm near Kansas City. As speaker, author, physician, and leader, Morsch believes in the power of service, and has dedicated his life to inspiring and mobilizing others to serve.

Dean Nelson, Ph.D., has traveled around the world, reporting for magazines, newspapers and other news sites. He has written about terrorism in Kosovo, slums in Mumbai, baseball in Dominican Republic, the Dalai Lama, religious persecution in Tibet, cholera in Haiti, contaminated water in Central America the America's Cup yachting race, and smuggling along the U.S./Mexico border; in addition, he has conducted writing workshops throughout the United States, Switzerland, Africa, and India.

Nelson has won several awards for reporting from the Society of Professional Journalists, as well as the top award from the CINE Society for a screenplay on AIDS. This is Nelson's ninth book. His first, *New Father's Survival Guide*, was about staying home during his son's first year. He has written for *The New York Times*, the *Boston Globe*, *Science & Spirit* magazine, *Sojourners, San Diego Magazine, Westways* and several other national publications. He holds a master's degree in journalism from the University of Missouri–Columbia, and a PhD from the E.W. Scripps School of Journalism at Ohio University in Athens, Ohio.

In addition to being in demand at writing workshops, Nelson speaks frequently at retreats. He is also the founder and director of the nationally acclaimed Writer's Symposium by the Sea in San Diego, where he has conducted interviews in front of a live audience with writers including Amy Tan, Anne Lamott, Kathleen Norris, Ray Bradbury, George Plimpton, Bill Moyers, Jim Wallis, Rick Reilly, Joseph Wambaugh, Peter Matthiessen, Donald Miller, Chitra Divakaruni, Roy Blount Jr., and dozens of others.

Nelson and Morsch's book *Heart and Soul: Awakening Your Passion to Serve,* won the San Diego Book Award. Nelson is the founder and director of the journalism program at Point Loma Nazarene University.

Dean Nelson and his wife Marcia, an accountant, live in San Diego and have two children. An avid hockey fan and player, he has not lost any teeth on the ice since elementary school.